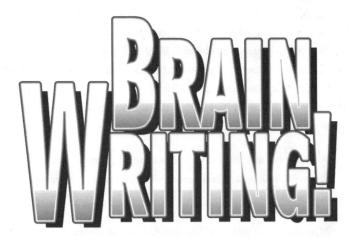

ENRICH YOUR LIFE USING HANDWRITING ANALYSIS

Irene B. Levitt

Brainwriting! Enrich Your Life Using Handwriting Analysis

Manufactured in the United States of America. Published by:

Serena Publishing
A division of Handwriting Consultants, LLC
480-661-9199

Publisher's Cataloging-in-Publication Data

Levitt, Irene B.
Brainwriting! Enrich Your Life Using Handwriting Analysis/Irene B. Levitt

ISBN: 0-9656723-2-8

1. Self-help 2. Handwriting Analysis 3. Health 4. Sales 5. Motivation

Editing: SageBrush Publications, Tempe, Arizona

Book Design, Illustrations & Typesetting: Running Changes, Phoenix, Arizona

Cover: Robb Pawlak

To

Gloria Bennett

Barriers

Behind closed doors,
many stand and wait impatiently,
hoping someone will lend them a hand
by bringing them a key.

At last, in despair, they turn and go,
never having knocked.

And they live and they die
and never knew
it wasn't even locked!

Author Unknown

TABLE OF CONTENTS

TABLE OF CONTENTS (cont.)

FOREWORD

I met Irene more than twenty years ago through our mutual interest and study of handwriting analysis. I have been a practicing Graphologist, also known as a handwriting analyst, for thirty-four years. My primary field is Forensic Document Examination, the identification of handwriting, such as forgeries, or the authenticity of handwriting. Irene and I formed a business partnership several years ago. She is an excellent handwriting analyst as well as a great partner.

In *BrainWriting! Enrich Your Life Using Handwriting Analysis,* Irene has done a wonderful job of explaining how your handwriting reflects your personality and your likely behavior pattern. She has shown how you can identify handwriting characteristics in your own handwriting. In addition, she reveals clues in others' handwriting that can assist you with your business.

It is my opinion that you will learn a lot about yourself and others through this innovative book.

Judith A. Housley, Document Examiner

PREFACE

As a music therapist, I worked with children who were emotionally ill. Later, I became a successful entertainment agent and casting director. Others viewed these careers as rewarding or even glamorous. After years of education and training, I switched to my new career as a handwriting analyst. I quickly learned that this often misunderstood job was an enigma. After meeting someone new and telling them what I did for a living, the typical response was, "You're a what?" accompanied by a face screwed up in puzzlement.

Then, there are others who hold their arms protectively about themselves (you probably are familiar with the usual body language sign) and say, "I don't want you to see my handwriting."

They needn't worry. There really is no right or wrong handwriting. Their writing exhibits their own wonderful uniqueness. Handwriting samples can double as seismographs of writers' feelings. Handwriting is an intriguing barometer of tendencies, strengths, and stresses.

You might ask, "Why bother to write by hand when the computer keyboard enables written communication."

When you write, you get in touch with your emotions and your intellect. Writing is an art form. All writing is good writing, because it represents your persona. It tells the story of who you are, what you are like, and what you are thinking. When you really want to get in touch with your thoughts or send a special note, always write it, personally, without the aid of a computer.

Thomas Gainsborough, one of the greatest of all English artists, achieved the lifelike quality of his portraits by having before him, while painting, a handwriting specimen from the subject. He felt that the handwriting enabled him to capture the very essence of the subject's personality.

Today many employers, worldwide, are hiring graphologists to use their skill to analyze prospective employees.

An Adventure into the Subconscious

Get ready to embark upon an adventure—an adventure into the subconscious. Before you read on, grab a piece of paper and a pen or pencil. Now, sign your name as you would on a check. Next, close your eyes (no peeking), and sign your name once more. Bet you're surprised! Everything you write comes from messages that are already programmed by your personality. If the only way you could write was by holding the pen in your toes or mouth, it would still look the same as it does now. Why? Because handwriting is really BRAINWRITING.

Your hand is merely a tool that holds a pen, while handwriting is the pen of the brain—a sort of x-ray that enables us to see what goes on in the body, mind, and emotions of human beings. When you write, you are not performing a simple physical function. The decision to write originates in your brain. The message is then carried along the nerve tissues down the hand and arm to the fingers, and you pick up your pen and write. As you write, you obey the guidance of your brain as it sends its orders through to the pen you are holding. As a result, handwriting is programmed by your brain. It could be called Brainwriting.

If the brain sends messages to your hand by way of your writing and suggests personality traits, why is it not possible to retrain some of those traits by changing your handwriting?

Handwriting analysis or graphology (the generic term) reveals a writer's personality and character. This book will show you ways to discover your inner self. Handwriting analysis can be a positive tool for self-understanding and self-development. In addition, it is possible to enrich your life by consciously reprogramming parts of your handwriting.

When you were in the third grade, you most likely began to write using the Palmer technique. You and your classmates tried to emulate your teacher's writing, but you rarely succeeded. The truth is that it was impossible for you to duplicate your teacher's exact writing style. Why? Even at that tender age, your personality had begun to invade your writing style. Your subconscious mind and personality traits were already beginning to influence what flowed from your brain to the pen and onto the paper. Many of us also were inhibited, to some degree, from allowing our own thoughts to flow with spontaneity and ease.

I remember my teacher, Miss Vincent, hitting my feet with her pointer as she walked up and down the aisles while we wrote. I often sat with my feet crossed at the ankles, and she would constantly point out this nasty habit by attacking my feet with her stick. My writing was always letter perfect. Now that I look back, it's small wonder. I had to conform.

Israel and the countries of Western Europe are highly advanced in their use of graphology. In the United States, libraries can't decide where to put books on handwriting. Only recently have Americans moved graphology books from the occult sections of the library to the psychology shelves.

There is no mystery about deciphering the written stroke. Handwriting analysis can help you understand yourself and others with keener insight. It worked for me—and my many clients. I know it can work for you if you'll follow the guidelines that I will share on the pages that follow.

INTRODUCTION

It all started the day I went looking for my first real job in Santa Fe, New Mexico. I had newly arrived in that sunny city with my husband, Phil; three very excited kids; our golden retriever, Buffy, and Tiger, the cat.

A perusal through the local newspaper, *The New Mexican*, told me that the Old Santa Fe Trail Association needed a part-time executive secretary. I was asked to complete an application and return in a few days to meet with the board of directors. I was told that they had narrowed the candidates down to two.

I felt encouraged when I met with the board. You can kind of tell when you have made a positive impact on a whole body of people. One person can mask his feelings, but a whole roomful of people usually is more truthful. I just knew I had made a good impression! I was in for quite a shock when the head of the board came out of the meeting room and told me that the job had been given to the other candidate. "Actually," he said, "The board was leaning toward you, but they decided to go with the other applicant." Then he turned to walk out of the room and added, almost as an aside, "I wish you had crossed your t's higher on your application." My t's? Good grief, what was wrong with my t's? I felt empty and slightly sick in the pit of my stomach. My first job interview in my new city, and I had blown it.

I soon realized that although it was the other woman who got the job—I was the winner. The bad news propelled me to new heights. The next morning, I hightailed it to our local library, searching for a book on handwriting. In 1974, that was not an easy find. Even today, most libraries boast few books on handwriting analysis. Santa Fe, a sleepy little city of barely fifty thousand souls was, at the time, just a little mountain hideaway in the Sangre de Cristo mountains.

Luckily, I found one book that told me that t's and t crossings were an indication of one's self-esteem, and my self-esteem couldn't have been much lower according to the handwriting evidence. My t-crossings were hovering toward the bottom of the stem and looked like this:

The book recommended that every night for a month I write a practice sentence using many lower-case t's. This sentence was to be written thirty times a night, preferably before going to bed. It suggested that I cross the t's as high up on the stem as I could, at least three-quarters of the way up.

I kept a pad and pencil on the nightstand, and every night I dutifully wrote lowercase, cursive t's, being very careful to cross the t's as high up on the stem as I possibly could but taking care to always touch the stem, as well. Willpower is observed in your t-crossings. I'll tell you more about that in Chapter Three.

After practicing for two weeks, I noticed
that I automatically crossed my t's at the top.
It was as if my subconscious had taken over,
and I did not need to think anymore about the
proper place to cross. I didn't know what this really
had to do with my self-esteem, but I was certainly
aware that I was now crossing my t's at the top. So,
BIG DEAL. But something had changed. Soon after,
I noticed that my handwriting was beginning to look
different. Then I stumbled across a sample of handwriting from when I was sixteen years old. It looked
like this:

thanks for the letter!

Good heavens, my t's at sixteen were always
crossed at the top! Even at ages seventeen and
eighteen, samples of writing showed t's smartly
crossed, right at the top. I began to wonder why my
handwriting had changed.

I married at the age of eighteen, then left college in my second year to put my husband through
law school. I began having babies and, little by little,
got caught up in the busy world of wonder wife and
supermom. I did all this willingly, without a regret at
the time. All of my friends were programmed from
birth to be helpmates to their spouses. At that
time—the fifties and early sixties—it seemed right. It
was everything I had been expected to do. What
happened, however, was that the direction my life
was taking had, little by little, been changing me. I

was never aware of these gradual changes until handwriting analysis BLASTED its way into my life.

I became compulsive about my study of handwriting. As I looked at anyone's handwriting, strokes began to jump out at me, especially mine.

For the first time, I began to see myself as I really was, and handwriting analysis was the catalyst. There it was, plain as day—graphic evidence that over the years, my feeling of self-worth had been gradually sinking lower and lower.

I learned that a good way to really look at myself was through this fresh perspective of handwriting analysis. I now had a new basis to understand myself without rose-colored glasses. This knowledge slowly began changing my life in the most positive way.

I had always enjoyed singing in musical comedies and began singing in local theater productions. There was time now to indulge in my passion to sing. My daughter, Sherri, and son, Rand, were grown, and our youngest, Rob, was just starting college. I sang with local little theater productions. My penchant for singing kept me at rehearsals and performances many nights. Soon my husband, Phil, became unreasonably jealous of my social contacts with others in the theater world, especially men. The majority of them were not interested in women anyway, but I had difficulty convincing him of this. Rehearsal time for me meant he spent most of his nights "out with the boys" at one of our local bars. He had always suffered from migraine headaches, but they became worse when he attended any of the productions in which I appeared. His distress troubled me.

At that time, my normal writing pressure was very light. Anyone who writes with light writing pressure feels just as intensely as those who write with heavy pressure, but only for the moment. She has a tendency to forgive and forget easily. (There's more about writing pressure in Chapters Five and Eleven.) My desire to please, indicated by light writing pressure, made it easy for me to forget my own desires to sing and entertain on stage. To please my husband, I left the world of amateur show business and became an entrepreneur. I started the New Mexico Entertainment Agency.

My agency represented musicians. I loved working in the business world. Besides, I reasoned if someone couldn't make his own gig, I could always fill in to perhaps satisfy my own desires to entertain. In seven years of running my company, I only filled in three times—each time, on Christmas Eve! I found jobs for talented musicians and also promoted major productions, booking and working with superstars like Johnny Cash, Doug Kershaw, Brenda Lee, and Buddy Rich. I was somewhat out of my element once when I booked the Chicago Knockers, a girl's mud wrestling group. After dealing with an unruly crowd, I decided to stick with only first-class music productions.

After two years of agenting experience, I learned that a Screen Actors Guild franchise had become available. Why not represent actors as well? The Hollywood Screen Actors Guild (SAG) agreed to issue me a franchise. A second division of my agency unfolded. I now represented actors.

Within a few months, I was asked to cast extras for a twenty-six-million-dollar disaster titled, *The Legend of the Lone Ranger*. Many local people had a chance to work on a movie set and, at times, I processed five hundred extras a day. It was exciting working with major Hollywood stars, and I derived much satisfaction in finding jobs for thousands of local folk.

The New Mexico casting for the award-winning miniseries *Lonesome Dove* was especially challenging and rewarding. It helped satisfy my penchant for working with many people. Yet the thought of understanding myself and helping others as a handwriting analyst continued to pull me in that direction.

I worked in casting for twelve years and continued to plug away on, first, the general course of graphoanalysis, then a resident degree, and, finally, after six years, a Master's degree. I envisioned myself as someday, perhaps around the age of eighty, analyzing little squiggles on paper. It could be my way to always remain a productive member of society. But why wait? Yet, the movie business was glamorous and exciting. I wasn't ready to give up the life of a casting director.

Then, on August 13, 1983, the unthinkable happened. My husband, Phil, committed suicide. It is difficult for me to write of this period. After the initial shock, I felt almost as if I were living in a surreal world. My life changed drastically. The kids' lives were ripped apart. This couldn't be happening to us. Our family was completely devastated.

Afterward, I tried hard to pick up the threads of our lives. Sherri had recently married, Rand was working in California, and Rob started his new life in Washington, D.C. I never felt more alone. I turned down requests to do castings. I felt down and depressed. Even my handwriting changed. I noticed my writing was very large, almost child-like. My overly large, light writing indicated a desire to be a little girl *child* and protected again.

The realization motivated me. I decided it was time to do something. I made a strong effort to write smaller and attempted to press harder on the paper.

Writing smaller helped me to gain back my ability to concentrate. Pressing harder forced me to find new energy and vitality from somewhere deep within. It helped to bring *new strength* me back to reality. Slowly, I began to feel better. When you smile, it changes the look on your face. I was helping myself to smile on paper.

I began looking for a way to travel alone. I impressed a cruise ship lecturer's agent sufficiently to give me my first chance to lecture on the Sun Princess, bound for San Juan and the islands of Saint John and Saint Thomas.

My initial attempt at lecturing about handwriting was fun. I enjoyed talking about a subject I loved so much, and, to my surprise, I liked being center stage in front of an audience. I had spent twelve years working on the task of getting jobs for others to appear in the spotlight, and now I was giving myself a turn.

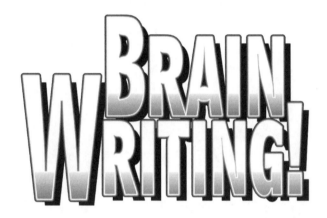

CHAPTER ONE

Chapter One
LEARNING ABOUT PEOPLE
THROUGH SYMBOLS

Being a professional graphologist and single presented its own challenges. After living alone for many years, I decided to date. Usually, on the first or second meeting, my date would write for me. Darn it, there were no surprises after that! And not too many dates, either.

Sometimes, though, I learned something about the "inner date" that I wouldn't otherwise have guessed. I once met a guy while I was playing at a doubles tennis match. We were matched as tennis partners, and we had fun playing together, but I didn't think we would date. He seemed nice enough, but I didn't feel that we had much in common. He kept sending me clever little handwritten notes. Pretty gutsy, don't you think, considering my occupation? I was impressed already. Actually, I observed that he was not at all what I had thought when I first met him. His writing told me that he was a pretty terrific guy, and sexy, too. We dated for a few months, and we're still friends, but my original intuition said, "This isn't gonna work for the long haul." To tell the truth, he was the first to say *adios*.

Every time I met a new guy, I thought about the potential for a long and lasting relationship. After many years of hopeful dating, I finally had to admit that Mr. Right probably would never exist for me.

And then I met Mr. Possibly Right (Where else? Another doubles tennis match.) The group was aptly named Unstrung Racquets. He seemed to have everything I was looking for in a mate—sensitivity, intelligence, and financial independence. My intuition told me that this guy, named Sheldon, looked promising. I thought smugly, I'll give him the acid test—observe his handwriting. He adamantly refused to write for me. He even laughed. "Why," he asked, "would I do that? You can read things into my handwriting and cut me off before we've really gotten to know each other. No, I want this to be as equal as possible. We can talk, but I'm not going to write for you. At least, not now."

By refusing to write for me, he took away my control. He removed the crutch I used to tell me how I felt about a man. He was forcing me to depend on observation, intuition, and feelings without my knowledge of graphology. I didn't trust myself, so how was I supposed to trust him? Perhaps he had something to hide! A tug of war continued between my heart and head. "He seems perfect for you," my heart said, "Why not give him a chance?" My brain chimed right in at that point, "Be careful. You're on foreign ground."

I was painfully aware of my own personality through handwriting analysis. Self-analysis revealed to me that I was likely to never love again because of past hurts. A small, quiet voice inside me asked, "Is that the way you want to live the rest of your life?" Of course, I didn't—but I still needed some way to evaluate Mr. Possibly Right. So, I used a backup plan.

A LITTLE DRAWING GAME

We played a little drawing game. I drew these four symbols for him on a paper napkin and asked him to pick the one that was most interesting. These are the symbols:

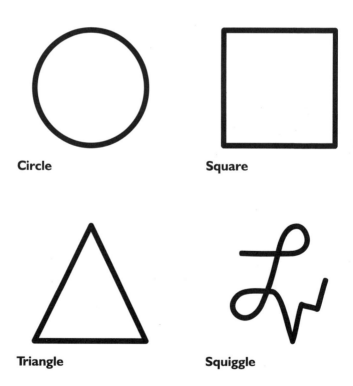

Circle   **Square**

Triangle   **Squiggle**

The Circle

I'll be darned! He picked the same symbol to which I was attracted—the circle. It meant that, to him, love was the most important element in his life. I knew that we had some of the same types of motivation in common. His choice told me that we were off to a good start. I was reasonably sure he was most stimulated by love and the desire to share his pleasures with someone else. Round forms in writing appear often in the o's, a's, e's, g's, upper and lower loops, and the letter-ending strokes.

His choice of the round form showed me that what he looked for mostly was affection and approval. By choosing the circle first, he shared the feeling that a love interest was the most important need for him. He could not happily be involved in his work unless he knew that he was sharing his life with a pleasing lady. Even though I couldn't see his writing, at least I had new knowledge with which to work. His choice of the circle first suggested that he would find arguments distressing and distasteful. What circle-first people seek most is affection and approval. Circle people are neither hostile nor aggressive. In short, they would rather play than fight. This information helped me to know, with no handwriting to back me up: "Mr. Possibly Right" was "Mr. Right." At our wedding ceremony, we simply spoke from our hearts.

Samples of Circle Symbols in Writing

Look at Linda Evans circle-like writing. Notice the heart-shaped I dot—an affirmation of her feelings and need for love.

Linda Evans, actress.

Jayne Mansfield, actress.

The Square

If Sheldon had picked the square first, I would have anticipated that order and discipline were most important to him. His priorities would be most evident in the letters h, m, n, r, p, u, and w. Square choosers are security-motivated individuals who like working with their hands and have a mind that likes to build on things. They enjoy the thought of puttering around the house. They are usually logical, practical and are the kind of person on whom one can count.

Samples of Square Symbols in Writing

Mr. Anagnos is away
and I am unable to get
appointed ticket; but I have
written two for you
which will do just as
well.
    Lovingly yours
        Helen Keller.

Please excuse this hastily
written note.
        Helen

Helen Keller, blind and deaf at nineteen months.

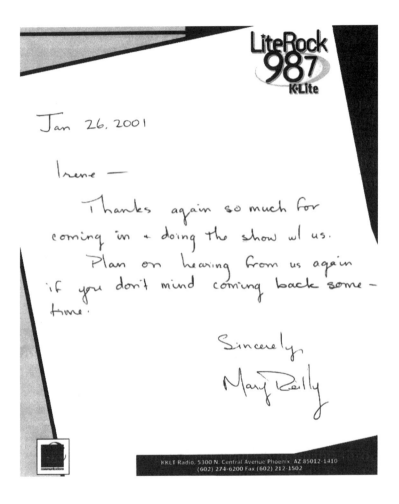

LiteRock
987
K·Lite

Jan 26, 2001

Irene —

Thanks again so much for coming in + doing the show w/ us.
Plan on hearing from us again if you don't mind coming back some-time.

Sincerely,

Mary Reilly

KKLT Radio, 5300 N. Central Avenue Phoenix, AZ 85012-1410
(602) 274-6200 Fax (602) 212-1502

Radio personality, Mary Reilly's first choice was the square.

From the Laboratory
of
Thomas A. Edison,
Orange, N.J. April 26 1914

Friend Ford

The injurious agent in Cigarettes comes principally from the burning paper wrapper. The substance thereby formed, is called "Acrolein".

It has a violent action on the nerve centers, producing degeneration of the cells of the brain, which is quite rapid among boys.

Unlike most narcotics this degeneration is permanent and uncontrollable.

I employ no person who smokes Cigarettes.

Yours

Thos A Edison

Thomas Edison, inventor and enterpreneur. Inventor of the light bulb. From the Collection of Henry Ford Museum & Greenfield Village.

The Triangle

If he had picked the triangle, I would have known the need for power was foremost in his personality. Actually, this was his second choice, and mine, as well. It is also the sex symbol. A pointed wedge shape can push further and release greater energy than any other form. Triangular letters show a sharpness of thought and keen perception, characterized by the wedge shapes and points that can appear in many letters.

Triangle people want to arrive at solutions quickly. They are independent thinkers and resist being placed in a subordinate position to others. They usually have a tremendous drive for achievement and are action oriented.

Samples of Triangle Symbols in Writing

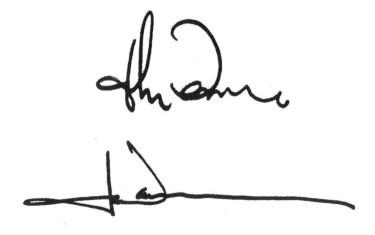

John Denver's signatures, musician and songwriter.

The first signature, written in the sixties, is circular; the second, written in the eighties, is triangular. This indicates a major change in his personality. The first example is evidence of his feelings of softness and love. Remember "Annie's Song"? The second example illustrates a life that changed, drastically, years later.

Colin Powell, Secretary of State.

Notice the triangle and also light writing pressure. Colin Powell once stated that he did not have the physical stamina to run for president. Please see Chapters Five and Eleven regarding handwriting pressure.

The Squiggle

If Sheldon had chosen the squiggle, imagination would have been his first motivation. The squiggle indicates a person with a need to create, one who rejects routine and who identifies the world about him, not just the society in which he lives. By combining all the other shapes, it creates a design of its own. When you do the same thing in your handwriting, you are using your imagination. The squiggle person rejects routine, punching a time clock, punctuality, protocol, and the sameness of activity.

Most squiggle people do not like to be closed in by boundaries.

Samples of Squiggle Symbols in Writing

The squiggle writing of Whoopi Goldberg, actress and comedian (notice the $ sign!).

Another sample of squiggle writing is Jim Carrey, actor and comedian.

It is rare to see a circle and triangle in the same signature. It would indicate two extremes to the person's nature. One is loving and playful; the other indicates a driving need to get ahead without emotional needs to slow him down.

Sample of circle and triangle writing of Garth Brooks, country singer.

I often find that couples who pick the same symbol have an interesting starting basis for a relationship. Usually, I see these symbols illustrated in their cursive handwriting. Don't despair if you and your lover pick different symbols. It is helpful, however, to understand the theory behind first and even second choices. Remember, opposites often attract and can be helpful to one another in compensating for the difference in each other's personality.

John Derek, movie producer.

Bo Derek, actress.

Linda Evans, actress.

Ursula Andress, actress.

The circular (need for love) movements are obvious in the signatures of Bo Derek, Linda Evans, and Ursula Andress. John Derek was involved with all three actresses. Although there is circular motion in his signature, his writing is the only one that demonstrates a triangle (power).

Pairs of Symbols Reveal More

Your second choice can be almost as informative as the first choice.

CIRCLE, then square:

Love comes first, but second is your need for security to ensure this love by keeping close around you home, family, and friends. You are not driven by a strong desire for money or worldly gains.

CIRCLE, then triangle:

Your major motivation is love, followed closely by the need for power and sexual expression. You can be playful and passionate with strong desires in both areas.

CIRCLE, then squiggle:

When it comes to love, you are an idealist. You look for love to satisfy all your passions and ideas. You are constantly searching for the perfect mate and will create the most imaginative method of finding that person.

SQUARE, then circle:

Once you feel safe and secure in your home environment, you will reach out for someone to share your "nest." Your family unit is the most important to you. A major concern for you is keeping the peace and maintaining harmony.

SQUARE, then triangle

Security is first and most important to you. If someone or something threatens your security, you will not hesitate to fight for it. Because you are bright, you will approach your problems with keen perception and a strong commonsense attitude.

SQUARE, then squiggle:

You might be a tough one to understand completely. First, you are a commonsense, practical individual who seems well grounded in reality. The other side of your personality indicates a frustration with routine and a desire for variety and change.

TRIANGLE, then circle:

You have a strong need to express love and are most motivated by sexual expression. It is important for you to surround yourself with people. You are action oriented.

TRIANGLE, then square:

You have the ability to look at a problem and tackle it without becoming too emotional. You approach most situations with a great deal of patience and understanding.

TRIANGLE, then squiggle:

You have a highly aggressive personality and are considered a unique individual. You are extremely creative and, for you, the "sky is your limit." You know no bounds.

SQUIGGLE, then circle:

Your imagination draws you to highly philosophical or spiritual pursuits. You are able to
envision beauty in all that surrounds you

SQUIGGLE, then square:

Although your home and environment is important to you, you find yourself thirsting for new
challenges that take you away from your secure environment. You are highly creative but endeavor to
keep a balance between your need for security at
home and your desire for adventure.

SQUIGGLE, then triangle:

You are highly creative and never stop moving.
Others would find it challenging to live with you
because of your desire for adventure and variety. It is
important for you to surround yourself with people.
You are action oriented.

It's a fun game to play with friends of any age.
During my lectures, I have given this test to literally
thousands. No one has ever disagreed with the initial
diagnosis.

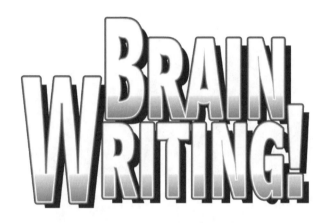

CHAPTER TWO

SIGNATURES

A signature is oftentimes the only sample you have of someone's handwriting. The word *signature* comes from a combination of two words—*sign* and *nature.* The signature indicates the way a person wants the world to see him or her. However, it may not be the way she really is. If possible, try to get a good look at the person's main body of writing. When the signature and the text, or main body of writing, are similar in size, spacing, and slant, then the writer's outward expressions reflect inner attitudes. Often she is saying, this is who I am—what you see is what you get. When the script and the signature seem similar, a writer is telegraphing that she is generally the same in public as well as in private.

During his campaign for president, George W. Bush sent a handwritten letter to his fellow Republicans. He was the only candidate to display his "writing." Other hopefuls running for national office, would only give their signature. In actuality, Bush seemed to be taking no chances that the body of his handwriting would be analyzed. Maybe the powers that be felt that it was difficult to read. According to television's *60 Minutes,* the Andy Rooney segment, the letter was digitally enhanced. Why did Bush not use his own script?

I face a challenge n
Republican does. I'm the /
The Clinton / Gore white Hou
Clinton is already attack
Other Republican Can
May resort to personal.
and negative ads.

Sample of President Bush's digitally enhanced letter.

In my opinion, the sample was a "cleaned up" version of his original writing style. His earlier writing showed an impatience with details.

Because I had been involved as a volunteer with John McCain's campaign, I hoped to get a sample of his writing. He refused, stating through his aides that he was concerned about an analysis of his personality and what the media might do with it. Perhaps handwriting analysis is more powerful than anyone will admit!

When you observe that the signature and regular writing are not similar, you can be sure that the individual wants to show one personality to the world at large but, in truth, has a different side to his persona. Often, you see a large, somewhat flamboyant signature with smaller, more concentrative writing.

Size of the Names

Here's another clue. To help put all the people puzzle pieces together, check the size of the names. If the first name is written larger than the last, you know the person places more significance on her own personal identity, which is separate from the family name.

Since a man rarely takes his wife's last name, I often see this sign in the writing of women. If a marriage has ended unhappily, a woman who keeps her ex-husband's name can subconsciously write her first name larger than she writes her last name. Many times, I notice an extra line drawn through the last name, an indication of the desire to obliterate the last name.

Grant Woods, former Attorney General of Arizona.

Michael Andretti, race car driver and son of legendary race car driver Mario Andretti. His writing indicates a strong will and a potential crossing out, or negation of self.

If the last name is written larger, the person places more emphasis on the spouse or father's name, rather than his or her first name.

Katherine Graham, editor and owner of The Washington Post.

When the signature is not legible, a writer consciously, or unconsciously, wants to keep his or her personal life private.

John Griffin, author of The Client.

Unusual Glitch

Handwriting analysis proved to be of great assistance when I was interviewed by an executive of the Disney studios to work as the local casting director for a hit comedy, starring Bette Midler and Shelly Long, called *Outrageous Fortune*.

The first interview was initiated via telephone. Rumor had it that the hiring executive was disagreeable to most everyone. When we spoke, briefly, he was somewhat sarcastic and argumentative. Fortunately, he followed up our conversation with a letter confirming an appointment. Of course, the letter was typed, but I struck pay dirt with his signature.

The executive's signature indicated a physical problem in the area of the stomach. Physical problems can often be observed in the handwriting. Glitches, unusual spots, or irregular pressure can indicate an organic problem. I could tell that my potential future employer had a problem somewhere in the central part of his body. I guessed that it was gallbladder trouble. It looked something like this.

(For more information on physical problems revealed in writing, see Chapter Four.)

When he and I met for our personal interview, I found him to be very testy and abrupt. Because I suspected he was in pain, it was easy to relate to him as if I were a sympathetic nurse. If I had not had this advance warning via handwriting analysis, I would not have related to him in the same gentle manner. It worked to my advantage—he was like putty in my hands. I got the job!

On the day we finished filming, I asked his personal assistant how the executive was doing with his gallbladder problem. Her shoulders stiffened, and her mouth dropped open. She asked me how I knew. She said he was always in great pain and was surprised that anyone was aware of his problem. I never told her that it came from my understanding of his handwriting.

Developing Your Signature

When you write your signature, you are creating the identity you want the world to see. Often, people who stylize their signature believe that it will be more difficult to copy. They purposely make it difficult or impossible to read. Many executives are concerned with signature forgery and mistakenly create signatures with easy-to-duplicate symbols, slashes, circles, or lines. In actuality, signatures that are not readily identifiable, may be easier to duplicate.

A difficult-to-read signature can be interpreted as a defense mechanism. These writers value their privacy and keep public and personal life separate. You will be perceived to be more trustworthy if the reader can identify your name.

MONTERREY, NUEVO LEON, MEXICO APRIL 22, 1993.

BY THE MEXICAN UNITED STATES

LIS SOCRATES RIZZO GARCIA
GOVERNOR OF THE STATE OF
NUEVO LEON

LIC. ERNESTO RUFFO APPEL
GOVERNOR OF THE STATE OF
BAJA CALIFORNIA

LIC. ELISEO MENDOZA BERRUETO
GOVERNOR OF THE STATE OF
COAHUILA

C. FRANCISCO BARRIO TERRAZAS
GOVERNOR OF THE STATE OF
CHIHUAHUA

LIC. MANUEL CAVAZOS LERMA
GOVERNOR OF THE STATE OF
TAMAULIPAS

LIC. MANLIO FABIO BELTRONES RIVERA
GOVERNOR OF THE STATE OF
SONORA

BY THE UNITED STATES OF AMERICA

THE HONORABLE FIFE SYMINGTON
GOVERNOR OF THE STATE OF
ARIZONA

THE HONORABLE PETE WILSON
GOVERNOR OF THE STATE OF
CALIFORNIA

THE HONORABLE BRUCE KING
GOVERNOR OF THE STATE OF
NEW MEXICO

THE HONORABLE ANN RICHARDS
GOVERNOR OF THE STATE OF
TEXAS

Whom Do You Trust?

Sample of NAFTA Agreement

The Life of the Party

Do you hate to make small talk at parties or business gatherings? Is it difficult for you to walk up to a stranger and introduce yourself? Or maybe it's just a bad hair day, and you're feeling a bit insecure. This technique will help if you feel timid or ill at ease.

Inevitably, you are asked to write your name on a name tag when you enter a room for a business or large social function. Write or print it as large as you can. Try to center your name without hugging the left side of the name tag.

Writing your name close to the left side of any paper when you don't need to conserve space indicates a withdrawal of self. Writing that clings to the left indicates a feeling of reserve or shyness. I used to do this all the time, perhaps giving some people the impression that I was aloof. In actuality, I was painfully shy.

When I went back for my high school reunion, one of my friends said, "Oh, we remember you. You were the one who blushed anytime someone spoke to you." I never told her that I was a recent past president of the Arizona chapter of the National Speaker's Association. In retrospect, I wish I had let her know.

Even now, I must make a conscious effort to remember to boldly write my name without hugging the left side of the name tag. I used to dread going to business cocktail parties. I never liked the little social games I felt I was obligated to play. I disliked talking to folks for only a few minutes, then moving on to another group of individuals to, once again, introduce myself. Invariably, I would leave early, and I'm sure no one even remembered that I had been there. I always had a terrible time and felt somewhat lonely. It was different when I changed the way that I wrote on the name tag that I plastered on my chest. I ended up having a really great time and feeling quite gregarious and cheerful.

In editing this manuscript, my editor added this note: I always have felt uncomfortable wearing a name tag that someone else wrote for me. On a subconscious level, I must have realized I was communicating something about myself that I preferred to communicate myself!

Play this little trick on yourself, and I promise it will help you to feel instantly more cordial and outgoing.

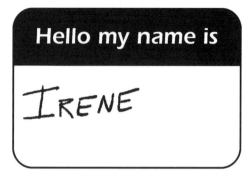

Writing showing insecure nature (hugging the left side).

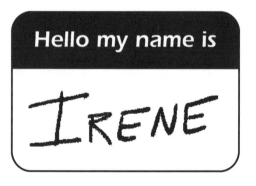

Writing showing outgoing nature (filling the whole badge).

Some Signatures of People You Know

Notice that each last name is written larger—a sign that they feel the strength and importance of the family name.

President George W. Bush, Jr.

Former Vice-President Albert Gore, Jr.

Former President Bill Clinton emphasizes his first name by writing it larger. He is demonstrating that he does not strongly identify with his family name.

Boxer, Muhammad Ali, formerly known as Cassius Clay, emphasized his newly adopted first name by writing it larger. This was written in 1964, just before the Sonny Liston fight. He rarely wrote Cassius Clay after that.

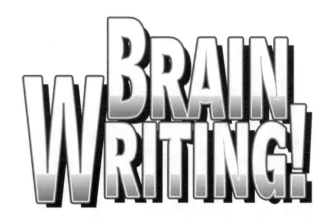

CHAPTER THREE

WHAT t-CROSSINGS MEAN

In the reading of handwriting symbolism, willpower is observed in the line that horizontally crosses the stem of the lowercase t.

That line is called the t-bar or t-crossing. The t-crossing is placed where the will is directed for that action. In most instances, the crossing reflects how high or low the writer's goals will be placed and how consistently they will be maintained. Observing the crossing of the t is a quick way to grasp an instant glimmer of a person's willpower or self-esteem.

Notice that I said glimmer. There are hundreds, maybe even thousands, of different types of t-bars when analyzed regarding the form and placement. Be careful not to read too much into your analysis of an individual by observing just the t alone. But when you are first beginning to understand personality traits, it is a good way to start.

The *weight* of the t-bar itself reflects the intensity of willpower that will be exerted in achieving a purpose or goal. The *placement* of the t-bar represents the attitude regarding the achievement of the goals.

The heavier and longer the pressure on the t-bar, the more intense the writer's will. I often find that when the t-crossing is especially long and heavy the writer's emotions are more in-tense. They are easily exhausted and will need time to recuperate—but, boy, do they get things done!

Conversely, a light and short t-bar indicates a less intense will.

Self-Esteem

When we write, we are strongly governed by our mind and the way our subconscious sees and feels things. If crossing your t's less than halfway on the stem feels good, and you are content with your job and your feeling of self-esteem, or self-worth, it would be folly to change.

However, many clients with whom I work who are advised to try to raise the placement of their t-crossing say that the exercise has added much to their feeling of who they are.

Leo Buscaglia said that "life is a process of un-learning...learning brings change...a person is introduced, finally, to himself." In handwriting, new learning and ideas can bring about great change. Negatives cannot survive if you don't feed them.

Jean Weber and Dr. Richard Stoller have done studies on the writing of school children in high school.

Jean, a graphologist from Phoenix, Arizona, is a teacher who has observed the writing of students with positive feelings of self-worth. She has documented hundreds of samples and has become aware that the students who placed t-bars low on the stem, were often the ones who did poorly on tests.

Dr. Richard Stoller, author of *Write Right: Change Your Writing to Change Your Life* and a high school principal, presented his doctoral dissertation on the psychological research of graphotherapy. Much of his book centers on the student's adjustment of writing style, especially when writing the lowercase t.

Even small children can benefit from learning to keep the t-crossing high.

The mom of a seven year old came to me complaining that her little girl never seemed to remember things she had to take to school. She also was a big procrastinator. In observing her printing (she hadn't learned cursive writing yet), I noticed the printed t-crossings were very low. I urged her to raise them, and she made a big effort to do so, with gentle reminders from her mom. Within a week after she began to practice her new t-crossing skill, a marked change was noticed. She rarely forgot items she had to take to school, and she began motivating herself to do more than she had ever done before, such as picking up her toys and helping her mother with chores.

If you consider yourself one of the many who are anxious to enrich your life and build on a new feeling of self-worth, then go for it! Be the person you want to be. Here's how to do it.

Try writing **take time to think** thirty times each night, using only lowercase letters, preferably before bedtime. When you sleep, your mind has a tendency to replay what happened just before bedtime. Although it's not necessary to do this exercise only at that time, it does seem to help the mind's absorption process. Be sure to do this every night for thirty days. You'll know when it becomes ingrained, if you see your t-crossings automatically rising higher and higher. Ideally, the t-bar should be at least three-quarters of the way up the stem.

More than self-esteem can be gleaned from the t-bar. Much can be uncovered about the personality from just that one stroke.

Willpower

The strength of your determination and willpower are observed in the intensity with which you cross your t's, both lowercase and capital. Your willpower is a trait that governs the effort applied toward achievement. The way you cross your t's indicates your strength of purpose. When you have a desire to achieve that is not strengthened by your willpower, it may not be powerful enough to withstand strong opposition. Therefore, a short, light t-crossing usually indicates a less intense willpower.

Once, in giving a lecture on the Royal Princess Cruise ship for a company's top sales group, a woman in my audience asked me about the hand-writing of the man sitting to her left. It seemed that he made all his t's like this:

The t-crossing was only on the right and usually didn't touch the stem.

I joked that she might consider moving her seat at the bar if this man next to her was drinking heavily. This t-crossing revealed the man had an explosive temper and, if provoked, could possibly let this potentially hot temper lead him astray. He admitted to this and, indeed, stated to our group that this was one of the major reasons he had decided to stop drinking many years ago.

The study of handwriting can often bring out some very traumatic, emotional responses.

During my lecture, I chose the word "mother" as an example of writing t's and asked the audience to write the word as they normally would. I don't know why I picked the word—it was the first one I thought of with a lowercase t. After my lecture, a woman from the audience came up to me with tears in her eyes. The writing of the word had a very special meaning. She noticed that she never crossed her t's with a dominating t-bar (slanted t-bar) except when she wrote that word. As she would write, she would involuntarily see and think of her mother. She explained, "My mother was very controlling, and since I was a very little girl, whenever I wrote that word, I always slanted the t. I guess now I know why." Thinking of her mother when writing that word triggered an automatic subconscious response. Her mind suggested control only when it involved her mother and, over the years, she absorbed this feeling and incorporated it into her normal writing pattern.

The t-crossing that is always feathered, or sharp ended, shows a tendency toward sarcasm. It often is demonstrated by people who have been hurt by excessive criticism, usually in early childhood. They have the need to be sarcastic as a defense mechanism—perhaps to hurt before they are hurt. The use of sarcasm in wit can be prevalent in this writer. The propensity toward sarcasm is shown in the slant drawn either straight across or pointed down. The significance is that it is pointed at the end.

One of my clients is a trust officer of a bank. He worked for years in the same position, never elevating his status at the bank. His t-crossings were usually particularly low on the stem. I suggested he try raising them. After about a month of concentrative effort, he announced to me that he didn't like the way he felt when he raised his t-crossings. Doing so always seemed to make him feel uncomfortable. I asked him, "Do you enjoy what you're doing at the bank?" "Actually," he said, "I really do, and I don't feel anxious about stepping up the success ladder. I like status quo." I suggested that he appeared content with his spot at the bank (as well as his life) and that, for him, raising his need for self-esteem was not a comfortable or necessary thing.

Your Technique Works

Recently, Marilyn Sprague-Smith, M.Ed., Training Program Director, Jamestown, N.C. wrote:

"You have a very powerful message in your book and it works.

"This past weekend, I returned to Chicago and participated in a Video Showcase. I felt so out of my comfort zone, but I knew I needed to do this. As I was preparing my material, I hand wrote each segment and totally focused on crossing the t's higher. You are right—it does alter one's attitude and it helped me feel better about what I was doing.

"A big 'thank you' for sharing this technique. It made a big difference to me at a critical moment..."

Elevating your feeling of self-worth by raising your t-crossing isn't necessarily always desirable. Depending on your present needs, lifestyle, etcetera, low t-crossings are not undesirable. Only you know. Ask yourself if your goals are being met.

Lowercase t-Crossings

1. Independence: short stem in comparison to other letters.

2. Enthusiasm: t-crossing slanting upward.

3. Tenacity: hooked at the end of t-crossing.

4. Sensitivity: looped t or d stem.

5. Dominating: t-crossing slanting down.

6. Domineering: t-crossing slanting down with sarcasm (feathered or pointed at end).

7. Persistence: tied crossing.

8. Dreamer, visionary: t-crossing that does not touch stem.

9. Lack of willpower, self-underestimation: low and light t-crossing.

10. Has willpower, but self-underestimation: low but heavy t-crossing.

11. Feels pressure from something or others: inverted umbrella crossing.

12. Self-control: umbrella-like t-crossing.

13. Procrastination: t-crossing does
not touch stem on left. Can also
be seen on the i dot.

14. Explosive temper: t-crossing does not touch
stem on right.

15. Stubbornness, decisiveness: tent-shaped
t-stem.

16. Increasing willpower: t-crossing ends heavier.

17. Simplicity, directness, precision: printed
t-stem.

18. Sarcasm: feathered or pointed end of
t-crossing.

19. Initiative: different ending, with no t-crossing.

20. Pride: tall t and d stems.

21. Deliberate in thought and action: curved,
separated t-stem.

22. Flowing, rhythmic, facile thinking:
t-crossing moves easily to begin
another letter.

Some Interesting t-Crossings of People You Know.

Bill Gates, executive of Microsoft.

He is feeling pressure from someone or something. Notice the inverted shape of his t-crossing. The loop in his t also indicates a sensitivity to criticism.

Frank Sinatra, singer.

Notice the high placement of his t-crossing, indicating a strong feeling of self-worth.

Bill Mariott, founder of the Mariott Hotel Chain.

This t-crossing does not touch the stem. It indicates a person who is a visionary, who envisions more than most people.

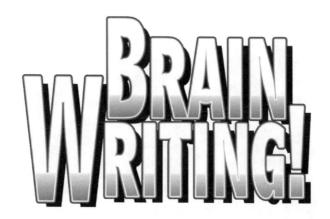

CHAPTER FOUR

Chapter Four
PHYSICAL PROBLEMS
The Symbiotic Relationship of Reflexology and Handwriting Analysis

I first discovered reflexology in an unusual way. After a particularly stressful incident involving a long-term relationship that had gone sour, I found myself suffering from a problem with my sciatic nerve area. I visited a doctor who specialized in sport injuries. When I was in his office, he did not question me about anything but the pain location. However, he did say something that I thought was unusual. "Take these pills, go home, and be good to yourself. Here's the telephone number of a good masseuse who specializes in sports massage."

He didn't have to say it. I suspected that he had intuited that my extreme discomfort was due to emotional stress. I'll bet he could tell just by looking at me. I was feeling like hell, and he might have guessed that the cause of my agony had begun because of a broken heart. My sciatic nerve pain was caused by extreme distress. "Hey, girl," I told myself, "Your torment is caused by the fact that you were just dumped." It was a reasonable assumption. It made sense to me. My love relationship had just been uprooted rather abruptly. My physical pain was caused by mental anguish.

The pain got worse. Soon, it was quite difficult to sit for even short periods of time. Driving a car became particularly unbearable. The pills prescribed by the doctor produced no relief from the pain. It didn't matter that I intuited what had almost certainly caused the problem. I needed a savior—a new love interest perhaps? Forget that. There was no one even remotely on the horizon. Besides, it was too soon for that anyway. The pain was getting worse. I needed immediate help—I was desperate for some relief! I went to visit the masseuse.

The masseuse suggested that I read books on reflexology and that I might relieve the pain by pressing on the correct pressure point. I left her office and went straight to the bookstore where I found tons of books about reflexology. From a simple diagram in one of the books, I found the point on the side of the ankle that corresponded to the area of my pain in the sciatic nerve.

Mostly, I was feeling great discomfort when driving. Whenever I suffered from the pain on the lower right side of my body, I reached down and pressed on the corresponding area of the left ankle. This was not too difficult because I did not use the left foot to drive. It was amazing to me that as long as I applied pressure in the correct spot, the pain on the right side subsided. Although it took weeks for the pain to fade away, pressing on the pressure point made driving tolerable

again. I became a believer! I had found a new best
friend—reflexology.

It is important to note that reflexologists and
handwriting analysts do not diagnose illness, nor do
they practice medicine. It is a matter of fact, however, that people who use reflexology attest to better
health and a marked reduction in pain or even dis-
appearance of the ailment. Don't give all the credit
to the reflexologist—only the body cures.
Reflexology can be a great aid to relieve some pain.

The Body Reveals Illness via Handwriting

The feet are a perfect microcosm or mini-map of
the whole body. I find it fascinating that it is possible
to relate to handwriting in much the same way. It has
become apparent to me that illness in the body often
shows up in handwriting.

Below is an illustration of the divisions of the feet and the areas of the body to which they correspond:

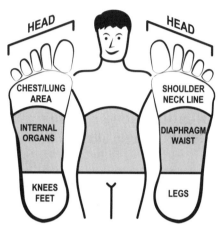

Notice the sections of the cursive letter f and the related areas in the body to which they correspond in handwriting analysis.

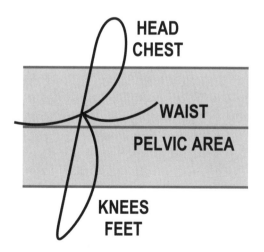

Reflexology is an ancient healing art. Basically, reflexology is accomplished by a gentle massaging of the foot at specific pressure points. In addition to acupuncture and acupressure, reflexology is one of the most convincing and applicable methods of controlling different types of pain and stress. Modern reflexology is both a science and an art. From ancient texts and illustrations, we know that the Chinese, Japanese, Russians, Indians, and Egyptians worked on the feet to promote good health.

Early in the twentieth century, Dr. William Fitzgerald developed the modern zone theory of the human body. He argued that parts of the body correspond to other parts and offered as proof the fact that applying pressure to one area anesthetized a corresponding area. Dr. Edwin Bowers, Fitzgerald's colleague, used a startling demonstration to convince others of the theory's validity. He showed that he could stick a pin into a volunteer's face without causing pain if pressure was first applied to the point in the person's hand that corresponded to that area of the face.

Much later, in the 1930s, Eunice Ingham, a physiotherapist for Dr. Joseph Shelby Riley, used zone therapy in her work with patients—this time, working with the feet! She discovered that the feet were the most responsive areas for working the zones of the body because they were extremely sensitive. Eventually, she mapped the entire body onto the feet and discovered that pressure on the various points had therapeutic effects far beyond the limited use to which zone therapy had been previously employed, namely, reduction of pain.

Even today, the actual physical mechanism that controls the various zones in the body and feet is not fully understood. However, it is thought that the feet are a mirror of the body, especially the soles of the feet. Each foot represents half of the body.

Handwriting analysis relates in much the same way as reflexology. There are relative zones in the writing that correspond to the zones of the foot.

A disturbance, or unusual mark of the writing, may be seen in a zone where it had not previously been observed. When there is a disturbance, (I like to call it a glitch or unusual mark) I often suspect a physical problem in that area. I noticed a change in my cursive writing of the lowercase g. Usually, my g is written like this:

After some particularly painful surgery on my right foot, I noticed a change in my writing.

Even though I was aware of the glitch, it would not leave my handwriting. Whenever I wrote, as hard as I tried, I couldn't stop the automatic insertion of the extra little glitch that appeared at the same spot every time I wrote the letter g. After about eight weeks, when the foot healed, the glitch left my writing. When my foot healed, the g looked like it always had, without the extra glitch.

Unfortunately, I do not think that it is possible to eliminate pain by consciously trying to remove a "pain glitch" in the writing. I tried very hard not to let the "glitch" become a part of my writing. No matter how aware I was, the extra "glitch" was an automatic, instinctive part of my writing. It did not leave until my foot was completely healed. Understanding handwriting can be a tip-off to understanding what is happening in the body. Writing helps to signal where in the body the problem might be. As the pain goes away, watch the writing for telltale signs. If healing is complete, the writing will usually return to normal. Relating it to areas of the foot is simply another way of grasping the accuracy of handwriting analysis. The brain, through your handwriting, is letting you know something is "off kilter" in your body. In my opinion, relating it to areas of the foot is simply another way of realizing the accuracy of handwriting analysis.

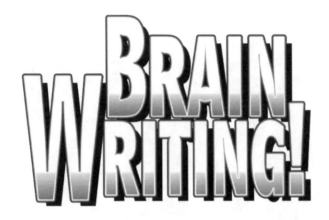

CHAPTER FIVE

EMOTIONS AND FEELINGS

To understand personality as a whole, it is necessary to completely explore the emotional structure of the writer. Your emotional makeup influences the effectiveness of all other traits.

A combination of the slant of the writing, plus the pen pressure (heavy or light), reveals the emotional foundation of an individual.

In his book, *Emotional Intelligence*, Daniel Goleman tells us how people of high IQ can have problems regarding their ability to think when their personalities are governed by their emotions. "Drawing on groundbreaking brain and behavioral research, Coleman shows the factors at work when people of high IQ flounder and those of modest IQ do surprisingly well. These factors add up to a different way of being smart, one he terms 'emotional intelligence.' "

Writing that Slants Up on the Page

Somewhere around fifth grade, we were learning to write without the aid of lined paper. I had a terrible time learning to write directly across the paper without constantly slanting upward like this.

upward slant I remember my dad spending many hours with me using a ruler as a guide to try to teach me the proper way to keep those words from climbing uphill. Try as I might, without the aid of a ruler it just wouldn't work. Everything slanted upstream—it still does. Writing uphill indicates optimism and enthusiasm. How excited I was to finally learn that upward-slanting writing was OK. Since the fifth grade, I always felt a sense of defeat when I had difficulty with writing directly across unlined paper.

If you are one of those people who could never keep an even keel to your writing without the aid of lined paper, take heart. Writing uphill can indicate a buoyant, upbeat spirit such as those illustrated in the following examples.

Oleg Cassini, the well-known clothing designer, shows much enthusiasm for life in his signature, written slanting uphill. Notice the heavy pressure, an additional sign of strength and energy. In addition, he underlines his signature. This is an indication that he is self-reliant.

Oleg Cassini, clothing designer.

Malcolm Forbes, founder of Forbes *magazine.*

Writing that Slants Down

Writing that slants down is often indicative of pessimism, depression, or sadness.

Robert Redford, actor.

Try writing any word, and make an effort to end it with a downward slant. Then, write the same word ending with a stroke that reaches up and toward the right.

If you notice your writing slanting down, make a conscious effort to swing upward with a forward movement.

Reaching out and slightly up toward the right can telegraph a feeling of optimism that sends an upbeat message back to your brain or subconscious. It is possible to elevate a sad mood by uplifting your writing.

Try it for yourself. Try writing words and finishing with a down slant. If this is not a library or borrowed book, write in this space.

How did you feel when you finished writing the downward stroke? In music, we would say it's like finishing on the downbeat instead of the upbeat.

Now, write the same words and finish with a slant reaching upward toward the right.

Can you feel the difference? Musically, it could be said that you were finishing on the upbeat.

Just the physical act of raising your ending stroke will, subconsciously, give you more energy. Ending most words to the right (without bringing the stroke back to the left) equals reaching out to others.

Writing to the right is reaching toward the future. This new conscious awareness of the ending stroke can help to elevate your mood.

I work with persons who have lost their spouses. Invariably, if their relationship was a fairly positive one, the loss sends them into a depressive mode, which is reflected by the downward spiral of their writing. Just the act of trying to consciously raise their writing can often help to change a despondent feeling into a more positive mode of thinking.

What the Slant Means

Your emotions are especially gauged by the slant of your letters, or strokes. The farther to the right your letters slant, the more emotional you are likely to be. Here's a helpful way to gauge emotions in writing.

How to Measure Slant

Measure only the upstrokes using the baseline as your frame of beginning reference. Observe the point at which you see the stroke begin to head upward and leave the baseline. Make a dot at this point.

Dot (a)

Now, follow the upstroke until it reaches its peak, before it starts its downward movement.

(b)

Dot (a)

Draw a straight line from point (a) to point (b). Continue this procedure for one whole line of writing and only measure the upstrokes.

Right Slant

If most of the strokes are slanted far to the right, you can assume that the writer is more affected by emotions than the writer whose slant is more vertical. The right-slanting writer is more sympathetic toward others. If the writing falls far to the right, the writer tends to be more impulsive and will leap before looking. When the writing falls far to the right in an extreme fashion, you might assume that the writer's emotions will lead into acts of strong impulsivity.

Burt Reynolds, the actor, has a far right slant.

It may be assumed that the feelings of right-slanting writers will rule their head, or thoughts.

The majority of people write with some sort of forward slant.

Vertical Slant

A vertical slant indicates an objective individual. This person can often appear reserved and is more likely to be head ruled, rather than heart ruled.

Donald Trump, entrepreneur. Notice, also, the many triangle shapes in his signature.

Left Slant

A slant to the left indicates a person who is more withdrawn.

This individual tends to be somewhat self-protective and finds more difficulty in "reaching out" to others. When the writing falls consistently to the left, the writer feels less need to be supportive of others.

Dear Mr. Lufalie,

Recently, I saw an article in the Buffalo News that detailed a man's arrest; one of the charges being "possession of a noxious substance" (CS gas). This struck my curiosity, so, I went to the New York State Penal Law. Sure enough, section 270 prohibits possession of any noxious substance, and included in section 265 is a ban on the use of "stun guns". Now I am a male, and fully capable of physically defending myself; but how about a female?

I strongly believe in a God-given right to self-defense. Should any other person up a governing body be able to tell another person that he/she cannot save their own life, because it would be a violation of a law? In this case, which is more important? Faced with a rapist/murderer, would you prefer to a.) die, a law-abiding citizen or b.) live, and go to jail? It is a lie if we tell ourselves that the police can protect us everywhere, at all times. I am in shock that ...

Timothy McVeigh, Oklahoma bomber.

Variable Slant

If the slant is not fairly
consistent, with most of
the slant looking
regular and fairly
rhythmic, you are
viewing the writ-
ing of a person
who is inconsis-
tent in responses.
When the slant is
not relatively even,
the individual is not
predictable. Erratic slant
that goes to the right and
the left in the same word can
serve as a red flag for other personality problems.

Pressure

Pressure is how hard or soft you press with the
pen or pencil.

It's a good idea to remember to use your knowledge of pressure because it's the easiest trait to spot
in a hurry, especially when looking upside down at
someone's writing. Yes, upside down. Sometimes you
only get a chance to read writing from farther away
that is upside down. It can often be very useful to
you. Think about it the next time you sit on the

opposite side of a desk or table that separates you from a person who is especially important to you for business or personal reasons. Try to observe snatches of writing on the desk that you are fairly sure may have been written by that person. There's usually one important piece of evidence that you can detect with only a quick glance—how HEAVY or LIGHT the pressure seems to be. Here's a sample of heavy writing:

Menendez brothers, convicted of murdering their parents.

The younger brother, Erik, was the controlling sibling.

I hope everyone has their fingers X. For me, I've Been working hard and I plan to Bring home a gold medal for U.S.

Tonya

Tonya Harding, ice skater.

Heavy Writing

Heavy writing indicates a deeply intense nature. Such writers carry feelings, hurts, or joys for a long time. If you see heavy writing, know that the person is probably self-assertive and determined. She usually has a very strong will and seeks to impose it upon others.

Compare Tonya Harding's writing to the medium pressure of the skater she caused to be hurt.

Nancy Kerrigan

Nancy Kerrigan, ice skater.

الى ايــُن الله ، ابنا الـساوى الذي خلقنا وخلق هـذا العالم والكون ـ ان
بنير العالم و امن هذا البيت بمالـيـه الذى يحطنا ايـها من اجل عالم افضل ولكى
نحصل على السلم ، والعادة الرا خلـق الذي اتنا هما لكن ستعـمها في هذا البيت ـ لاولادهم
ولاولاد اولادهم في حياتنا التى نقضيها على هذه الارض .

Sadam Hussein has more than the usual determination. Compare the writing above to Hussein's. It
is the even, rhythmic, and disciplined writing of an
Arab scholar.

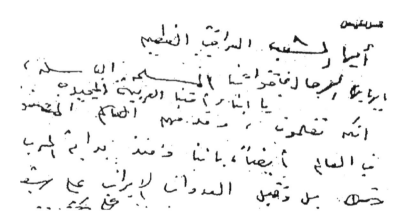

*Sadam Hussein's writing is that of an explosive and
violent man.*

*The Arabic signature of Muhammad Ali shows a calm
temperament.*

Now, stop for a moment, and try writing your name as you would on a check, but press hard on the pen. Find a separate sheet of paper if this is a library book or it is borrowed.

Notice that you cannot exert heavy pressure unless your muscles are tensed or contracted.

Heavy writers have feelings that are more intense than the average, and heavy pressure indicates an assertive personality.

Light Writing

Now, write your name a second time, but do not press hard on the pen. Try to be aware, while you are writing, of how you feel when you write with a light stroke, versus the way you felt when you pressed hard on the pen using a heavy stroke the first time.

Light writing indicates a nature that may seem to ignore hurts or pleasures. The writer initially feels joy and sorrow just as intensely as the heavy writer but only for the moment. A light line writer can be just as hurt or pleased as a heavy writer, but the emotion does not usually leave as lasting an impression on the subconscious. I find persons with light writing may be more relaxed and possibly more passive. They are usually more spiritual than assertive.

Lily Tomlin, comedienne and actress.

'A- KID ON THE BLOCK "

I was definitely a light line writer and was unhappy when I became aware that I glossed over problems and life in general. I made a special effort to press heavier on the writing instrument. I searched for pens that seemed to allow me to write with a heavier line. Even though I probably did not press much harder than I was used to, it felt more solid and substantial to me. I found myself becoming gradually more assertive and positive about where I wanted to go with my life.

I do not espouse this theory as a definite step for all light line writers. To assist my own growth pattern, I needed to stop reinforcing old habits, such as giving in to others most of the time. I disliked arguments and would do most anything to avoid them. That is also a trait of most people who pick the circle symbol first. Pressing heavier on the pen became a new part of my growing process. If you are a light line writer and feel the need to change from a forgive-and-forget attitude, it won't hurt to try. If it doesn't feel comfortable, don't continue to reinforce the more intense, heavy script.

Always use the writing instrument that feels comfortable to you. Using a pen that inhibits your natural writing style can throw you "off kilter." If the pen or pencil doesn't feel right, you will feel uneasy or discombobulated. It can temporarily make you feel off balance and be unsettling to your sense of well being.

If there are only two handwriting traits you remember, remember PS (pressure and slant). Learning to observe merely the pressure of the writing and the slant will help to go a long way in your understanding of personality.

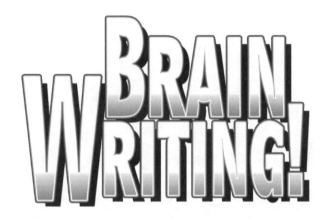

CHAPTER SIX

Chapter Six
UNCOVERING A HIDDEN
PERSONALITY TRAIT

Repression: "The fear of expression causing painful impulses, desires, or fears to be excluded from the conscious mind."

After I felt I finally had a good start with my high t-crossings and increased writing pressure, I began to feel an exciting new surge of confidence and started to search for other signs of self-worth.

Good grief! It was truly a shock when I discovered that a big part of my personality was governed by repression!

Repression is indicated in the handwriting by the retracing of strokes. You can see signs of repression when an upstroke retraces a downstroke. This retracing indicates repression of feelings or thoughts.

noun   mom

I know, by now, you must be thinking, "but that's the way I was taught to write." Well, you were absolutely correct. Without being aware of the consequences, the Palmer method taught us to reinforce our need to hold back our feelings. What we actually were reinforcing, to a large degree, was the stifling of our inherent mental acuity.

Try writing the word, man, and make an effort to retrace. *man*

You actually have to slightly slow down the writing process, ergo the thinking process, to conscientiously overlap the downstroke with the upstroke.

In reality, what is accomplished through repeated writing practice, with constant retracing, is the establishment of a pattern. This pattern, reinforced through writing every day, presents a constant pounding away on the subconscious and affects control by eliminating the unbridled freedom of thought.

Many of my peers, especially males, learned naturally to rebel against this and often unjustly received poor grades in penmanship in elementary school. In the fifties, most boys were brought up to think of themselves as the primary wage earner and family provider. Because of this, they usually lived with fewer controls, at home and at school. They were encouraged to use their intellect and wits more so than girls to make their way through life. They enjoyed more freedoms and were less inclined to conform as much as the girls did. Although they tried just as hard as the girls did, often it was impossible for them to write just as their teacher did.

Today, handwriting is sexless, even though our society is still basically male dominated. Forty years ago, sexism existed because women were, in many instances, thinking in a restricted, and clinging-vine fashion. The woman's place was in the home—as a dependent of the provider. Certain personality characteristics, attributes, and professions were considered strictly feminine and others strictly masculine. Today, women have invaded almost all fields that once were considered exclusively male provinces. Men and women think very much alike; the matter of sex is secondary as far as mental expression of identification is concerned.

When I observe handwriting today, even though there is no difference between most strokes, I still see more signs of repression in women than in men.

Through the study of handwriting analysis, I discovered late in life that what I was practicing (or what was practicing on me) was controlling my natural ability to think in an uninhibited way. I slowly began changing the retracing stoke.

This is a sample of the writing I did before discovering the *think* repression stroke.

This is a sample of my writing after eliminating the repression stroke.

I must confess that, at times, *think* repression still creeps back into my writing (old habits die hard). But, that's alright. When I become aware that I'm slipping into an old pattern, I merely try to not retrace—and it feels good.

The act of repression inhibits the ability to use native intellect. We were all born with much more capacity to think than we actually use. My resistance to retracing enhanced my ability to think with sharpness. My mind was being trained to move faster because my subconscious was being reprogrammed.

If your self examination shows no retracing of m's, n's or h's you probably are not feeling the tight controls with which those of us who retrace can get entangled. If you do retrace and you are aware of feeling repressed, make an effort not to retrace strokes. It could be the first step toward relaxing and, therefore, releasing your thought processes. Try writing words cursively, and be conscious of how much or how little you retrace. Even a small amount of retracing can be improved. This practice, once again, can best be accomplished just before bedtime.

Repression is the process by which individuals, through repeatedly denying their thoughts or feelings, drive these emotions out of their conscious mind into their unconscious, where they are no longer aware of their influence.

Repression, in itself, is not always bad. Sometimes the act of repression can save a situation from which we cannot immediately extricate ourselves, such as a bad marriage, but it is usually only temporary. When life becomes difficult, we can stuff our feelings and pretend that the problem doesn't exist. We don't have to see because we are unable to see. Repression can dull the intellect and usually does. It can even cause physical problems, as well.

Repression in writing indicates unconscious fears that can prevent you from reaching your full mental potential. When you consciously try not to retrace, you are enriching the realization of your plans and desires, especially those that affect your everyday living. If you eliminate retracing as much as possible, you will enhance your ability to be freely self-expressive.

Even if you have difficulty in practicing effectively, keep at it. It will take a bit of effort, but you will soon see that it is worth it.

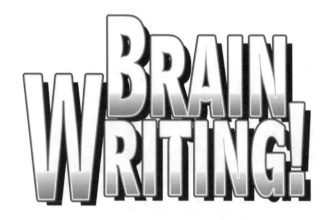

CHAPTER SEVEN

CONCENTRATION

Concentration is defined as "the ability to center attention to the exclusion of other interests."

The troubled mother of a twenty-one-year-old son complained to me that her son wrote using only very small letters. She sniffed, "He has always been an underachiever, so his writing shows me he must have low self-esteem." She was surprised when I told her his writing was well organized and showed his innate ability to concentrate.

In some cases, condensed writing, if the script is poorly organized, could suggest lack of confidence, shyness, and a tendency to focus on a small, inner world. Usually, however, the tendency to write small indicates a person who has the ability to concentrate.

Natural concentration, if present to a marked degree, affects all other traits shown in the writing. For example, if jealousy occurs in the writing, along with concentration, the intensity of jealousy will be greater.

Jealousy is observed when there is a small loop at the beginning of the capital M, N, or W.

M N W

What a pity that the writing of capitals with small loops was encouraged when we were first learning to write in grade school.

If we enlarge those initial loops, we indicate the desire for responsibility.

$$\mathcal{M} \quad \mathcal{N} \quad \mathcal{W}$$

Think back to your first grade school experience of learning to write cursively. At first, everyone in the classroom tried to emulate the teacher's writing. At the end of one month, not one child could write exactly like that teacher. Most kids were unfairly graded for their inability to duplicate the method of writing they were trying to copy. Even in third grade, that young emerging personality needs freedom to use its own style.

In his book, *Write Right: Change Your Writing to Change Your Life,* Dr. Richard J. Stoller tells the story of how teachers actually encourage their students to concentrate less by discouraging small writing. They tell their students who write small to write bigger, thereby lessening the native ability of that child to think in the way that is natural for her. In a way, students were "forced" to write larger, especially if they wanted to get a good grade.

Here's a test especially appropriate for medium to large writers. Use the space in your book to write your name as you would normally, then write it again, only smaller. Now write it a third time even smaller.

Notice how you feel as you are writing the third time. In addition to feeling perhaps more tense, or tight, you probably were aware of being more focused.

Large writers can often be good salespeople because they seek and enjoy people. A busy social life is important to them and helps gratify their inner need for recognition. They usually have a desire to be important. It is easy for them to mingle with a variety of people.

People find that when they take notes at a lecture their writing often becomes smaller, without their even thinking about it.

If you do not normally write small, learning to write in a more concentrated way can be a help before speaking or doing anything that is important to you. If you are making an important presentation, taking the time to write, even for only five minutes, can help you become more centered and keep your mind on track. The writing should be done as fast as is comfortable, without trying to make it look too perfect.

I am a medium-size writer. Whenever I need to make an important speech or presentation, I try to take the time to sit down, preferably about a half hour before I must make the presentation, and write smaller than I usually do. This smaller writing helps me to focus completely upon the work at hand and usually intensifies my ability to keep my wits as sharp as possible to handle the important task of that hour.

I am asked to be a guest on many radio shows. The listening audience is invited to fax a small sample of their handwriting to the radio station. I have approximately five seconds to look at the handwriting and indicate over live radio a few of the writer's personality traits. After I state a few handwriting facts about the individual, that person is invited to phone the station, and then we have a three-way conversation between the caller, the radio commentator, and me. It's a safe bet to say that I'd better be sharp, or it could be quite embarrassing. After many radio broadcasts, I have never had a listener call to say that I was wrong. I ALWAYS write very small for a short time before going on the air. I know this helps to keep my mind sharp.

Have you ever noticed a bookkeeper's ledger? It is made up of small squares. Have you ever wondered why these squares are so small? A long time ago, a very astute printer of ledgers noticed that his own bookkeeping was more accurate when he made the squares smaller. He didn't know why this occurred, but he was aware that he sold more ledger books when the squares were printed smaller. Other printers followed suit, and now all ledgers use small spaces to record figures.

Your ability to concentrate increases as your writing becomes smaller. It stands to reason that by forcing yourself to write smaller, you will remember more of what you have written and make fewer errors.

You are reaching into your subconscious by writing smaller. It becomes easier to pull out more information. The conscious mind uses only five to ten percent of the entire mind area. Why not reach into the other ninety to ninety-five percent of your brain?

In general, writers who normally write very small are highly concentrative individuals who usually pay more attention to detail and are not among the more talkative members of a group or association. They are inclined to be modest and usually don't require lots of attention. They are also somewhat selective of friends, interests, and activities.

One of my students suffered from a brain injury, due to an automobile accident. Her writing was fairly large, and she reported feeling anxiety, especially when she wrote. Writing smaller proved to be a big help. She has told me that she feels "calmer and more relaxed" when she takes the time to write smaller.

10.

I write small. I calm down. My heartbeat is down and my brain is not jamming. Thanks

Student's statements in her own hand.

President Ronald Reagan wrote this note to me shortly after his illness was diagnosed. Notice the size of his normal signature versus the subconscious shrinking of his writing when he penned this letter. He innately knew he had to concentrate more intensely, ergo, his writing shrank.

RONALD REAGAN

D ear Friend:

    Nancy & I are deeply grateful for your kindness following the announcement of my illness. Individuals like you give us the courage and inspiration to move forward. With your prayers and God's grace, we know we will be able to face this latest challenge. May God bless you.

    Sincerely, Ronald Reagan

11000 WILSHIRE BOULEVARD
LOS ANGELES, CALIFORNIA 90024

Ronald Reagan

Former President Ronald Reagan.

For years, I have worked with "at risk" children in the inner city of Phoenix. I have found that asking them to write smaller when they want to concentrate on a task, has paid off with big dividends for the writer. The following sample is a teenaged boy's writing. He was in jail after writing graffiti on many buildings in his neighborhood. I was asked by the local authorities to work with him, and others like him, to try to reduce their desire to show power by defacing public property. Notice the triangle-like shape (desire for control and power) of his printing. He was so carried away with his artistic effort, that he was unable to spell all the words correctly. When requested to write smaller, increasing his ability to concentrate, he began to print in a more normal fashion. He even demonstrated that he really knew the correct way to spell all the words.

I ARLOO
RUEZ

NOT STUCK UP

ALWAYS HAS SOMETHING TO DO

FUNNY

I Don't know what else.

TAKE TIME TO THING

take time to think

Teenager's graffiti-like writing.

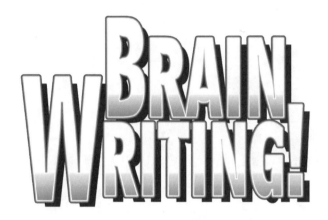

CHAPTER EIGHT

DECEIT AND HONESTY

Dishonesty is the unconscious expression of a person's deficiency in the area of basic integrity. It results from a lack of moral and intellectual qualities that enable one to withstand excessive ambition and the craving for power, luxury, and acquisitiveness. Deceit is often associated with a general preoccupation with material goods or glory.

I believe, however, that it is possible for any person to be deceitful if placed in a stressful situation. For instance, if I did not have any money and my children were hungry, I would probably be highly tempted to steal food in any way that I could. Most probably, I would ask to work for it first; but if that were not possible, you bet I would take the only option that I had—become a temporary thief. There are ways to look at handwriting to perceive certain characteristics that make people more prone to cheating to achieve what they want.

A wealthy friend had hired a housekeeper and cook. She did her job admirably and was rewarded with a lovely Mercedes sedan. They had a warm friendship, and he never dreamed that slowly, over the years, the housekeeper had been milking his bank account. He would write checks for groceries with all of the numbers hugging the left side. They looked like this:

*NINE*_____dollars

The devious lady would add this to them:

*NINE HUNDRED*_____dollars

He was puzzled and hurt when the situation came to light and asked me to look at her handwriting. I saw her shopping list for the day.

eggs
butter
bread
apples
milk

In her writing, major hooks in front of every initial word showed a strong desire to acquire.

Most often, those businesses that suffer dishonesty through embezzlement of funds find that employees have worked for them for a number of years before they begin their path of deceit. There are five main traits in handwriting that indicate embezzlement. Those traits are:

- vanity

- resentment

- imagination

- sensitivity to criticism

- a cool nature

Vanity Vanity is indicated in large loops in the writing of capital letters. The initial capital letters will be more than two and one-half times the lowercase letters in size.

Resentment is shown in the inflexible stroke of a beginning letter in the lowercase word. → *resentment*

Sensitivity to criticism can be indicated by heavy writing and/or looped d's or t's. *d t*

A cool nature is indicated by an upright slanting of the letters. *cool*

It often takes three to five years to catch embezzlers. A cool nature and intellect tend to keep them one step in front for a long time.

The ability to determine traits of honesty through handwriting analysis is not innovative. Many banks and insurers all over the world have used this skill, including Lloyd's of London. It can be especially helpful before bonding or insuring employees who must handle large sums of cash.

It is not possible to say without a shadow of a doubt that someone will steal, cheat, or be dishonest. It is possible to say that a person has a strong propensity to be dishonest if given the right motivations or conditions.

Frankness is the inclination to be sincere and forthright in communication. It is rare indeed to see complete frankness, because that means that the individual is totally free of secretiveness, evasiveness, or outright deceit of others.

Secretiveness is seen in the upper loops of circle letters.

Deceit of others would display loops of circle letters on the right.

Self-deceit is indicated with loops of circle letters on the left.

In judging frankness, it is often helpful to see an open e, which indicates an open feeling toward others.

The handwriting analyst is called upon to carefully study and evaluate form, spacing, connections, pressure, speed, and rhythm, but you, as a layperson, can certainly train your eye to look for particular alarm signals. A strong indication of integrity is the absence of embellishments or artificiality in the writing.

The basically honest person's writing will show most of the following traits:

- Clearness

- Legibility

- Uniformity of style, especially in the middle zone

- A firm baseline (but not rigid)

- Consistency in slant and consistent, clear spacing.

Consider Jimmy Swaggart's writing.

The first signature was his normal signature when he was in his heyday as a television evangelist. Notice the big circle covering up his last name. The second sample came after his cheating was uncovered. He dropped the cover-up

circle (also a love symbol). The signature shows a wavering of his sexual nature in the quivering line of the g's. I'll tell you more about the sexual area in ChapterNine.

O.J. Simpson,
professional football
player tried for the
murder of his wife
and her friend.

O. J. Simpson's writing shows signs of deceit, especially when you observe the circle letters. Notice the extra lines in his O. Here are three signatures. The first, he gave to a knife dealer three weeks before the killing of his wife and her friend. The second, he wrote to a young boy who attended his daughter's dance recital the night of the murder. The third is his signature on the "suicide note," written after the famous car chase. Notice the smiley face and the simple printing of O. J. A smiley face? Can you imagine drawing a smiley face after suffering such a trauma? This is an indication that he felt separate from the whole incident. It is a classic example of a dual personality.

Another example in the writing of the murderer of Bill Cosby's son. Observe, once more, the smiley face.

about the hate. there was no partner
I went to rob a connection, but
obviously found something else. ☺

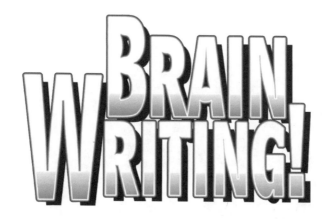

CHAPTER NINE

SEXUAL VITALITY

Emotional intensity and physical vitality are important qualities that help determine sexual forces. Pressure is an especially helpful measuring tool to assist in determining emotional intensity and physical vitality. It is difficult to achieve positive sexual energy if one is not in good health.

Erratic Pressure

Elvis Presley, King of Rock n' Roll.

Erratic pressure indicates an energy that is not consistent. It illustrates some anxiety or tenseness and, possibly, ill health.

Light Pressure

Christian Slater, actor.

Pressure that is gossamer-like indicates a delicate and/or a superficial feeling.

Heavy Pressure

Sean Connery, actor.

This sample is indicative of great emotional and physical energy.

Very heavy pressure, especially when the stroke digs into the paper, exhibits frustration and internal inhibition.

ZONAL AREAS

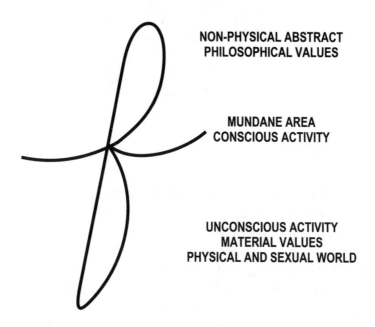

**NON-PHYSICAL ABSTRACT
PHILOSOPHICAL VALUES**

**MUNDANE AREA
CONSCIOUS ACTIVITY**

**UNCONSCIOUS ACTIVITY
MATERIAL VALUES
PHYSICAL AND SEXUAL WORLD**

There are three zones of which to be aware when observing handwriting. When the zones are balanced, with the ascenders, middle section, and descenders in proportion, the writer's emotions are more likely to be expressed equally with mental, social, and physical aspects all playing the same part.

The upper area represents the non physical/abstract philosophical values. When the writing extends far into this area, the writer's thinking leans toward the highly imaginative. The upper range of thinking extends into the realm of religion, philosophy, and, perhaps, politics. The approach of such writers is largely theoretical. Their philosophy of life appears broad in scope, and they view life through a wide-angle lens, which can encompass many theories.

Deepak Chopra, M.D.

If the upper zone is dominant, (very tall, wide, or embellished) the focus is on fantasy, spirit, or intellect. The mental world dominates.

If the writing does not seem balanced by the lower area, with some lower extensions, you may assume that the writer is interested in learning for its own sake, but has a problem putting what she learns to work.

The central area of the writing is representative of the conscious, everyday thoughts of the writer. If the middle zone (mundane area) dominates, the writer's most emotional energy is spent on personal needs, daily concerns, and social interactions.

THANK YOU FOR PROVIDING

IT WAS GREAT SPENDING

If the mundane area does not extend up into the abstract or down into the physical world, the writer's philosophical approach to life may be restricted to realistic concepts.

His or her interests are more likely ideas that appear practical or realistic. If the writing is concentrated in only the mundane area, the writer may find it difficult to appreciate creativity in others.

Revelations of the Cursive g

The lower area of the writing represents unconscious activity, material values, and the writer's physical and sexual world. It is considered the action area. The lower area represents the active imagination of the writer. Of all the letters that pertain to the attitudes and concepts of sex, the small letter "g" is the most revealing.

Here are some samples and explanations of the cursive g:

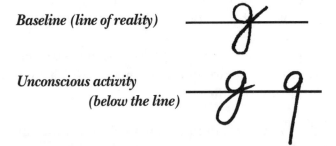

Baseline (line of reality)

Unconscious activity
(below the line)

The letter "g" represents our attitude based upon past experience. The lower loop reflects feelings that are formed from past relationships and symbolizes one's identity with others. The writer makes a decision by going down into the unconscious then brings that feeling to the surface, or baseline. The baseline is the line of reality. The larger the down-stroke, the more energy that is shown. When the lower loop goes straight down, loops and crosses over, it is considered "normal." After years of re-search, this stroke reveals, with an amazing degree of accuracy, many sexual proclivities. A word of cau-tion: It is best to look at more than a few examples before making a judgment. In my estimation, this letter represents the law-of-the-jungle sexual vigor and energy. The formation of the letter reflects why the writer feels about himself as he does. Handwrit-ing changes when situations change, so be careful not to make a snap decision when observing this trait in the writing—it can be downright dangerous.

g Stroke that resembles copybook g: shows har-monious integration of parental values and experiences

q Round circle with straight downstroke: good at delegating but leaves the follow-through to someone else. Not capable of completely relating to feelings.

This writer uses energy in a business career and very often displays good judgment and a fatalistic attitude toward life.

8 Figure "8": fluidity of words and actions; moves easily from one project to another.

9 Angle in lower loop: needs to control any relationship, cannot relate to feelings.

Disappointments with the partner result in aggressiveness caused by frustration.

If female, this writer is boss of the house; if male, he is a man who demands his sexual rights and will see that he gets them, even if he has to use brute force.

  If the lower line leans to the right, the writer was highly influenced by the father.

OFFICE OF THE MAYOR
CITY OF CHICAGO
February 9, 2001

Sincerely,

Mayor

Richard M. Daley, current Mayor of Chicago.

If the lower line leans to the left, the writer was highly influenced by the mother.

ℊ Downward ending: discouragement, depression, or anger toward current sexual partner.

ℊ Retracing: repression of sexual and emotional needs.

ℊ No downstroke at all: Writer lives in an emotional vacuum. Incomplete in the sexual area.

ℊ Very small loop at the end of stem: shows the loner, the solitary person who may be sexually frustrated.

ℊ "Glitch" in circle g: disappointment in past love relationships that can affect future relationships.

ℊ Lower loop slanted to left: feelings controlled by past experiences and female figures.

ℊ Lower loop slanted to the right: feelings controlled by hope for the future and male figures.

q g Long, heavy and looped: strong physical desires and appetites.

When the lower extender is long, the writer's need for variety is intense. If the lower loops or sticks are the longest or fullest shapes, then the emotional focus is on the instinctual self or the physical body. The writer's energy is expressed in drives for security, sex, or money. She feels the need to escape from the routines of daily environment and is inclined to keep herself occupied with many varied activities. When bored by mundane living, she tends to search for excitement in change and needs the stimulation of different friends and experiences.

9 Narrow or thin strokes can be a sign of physical illness.

9 Emotional immaturity, incomplete in the sexual area.

If the lower sections of your letters are not particularly long, and your partner's writing is elongated (or vice versa) you might have a few questions. No need for concern. A writer with an extended lower area can be faithful to one person and can come up with interesting scenarios that might keep a partner's attention long past the honeymoon stage of a relationship. Be aware, however, if that sexual need is not fulfilled, the partner could become restless and might feel a great deal of stress.

Nancy Reagan, first lady—no lower extenders. All of her physical energy was enabled through President Reagan.

John Wayne Bobbitt became infamous due to his wife's use of a knife that cut off a vital part of his body. Here, he incorporates his signature with this unique drawing that looks suspiciously like a knife. He seems to have positioned it in just the exact place.

Remember, a little bit of knowledge is a dangerous thing. It is folly to try to judge an individual by just one or two indicators, especially when you are a beginner in the study of handwriting analysis. For those readers who desire more information, there are a few books that address the area in detail, such as Karen Kristen Amend's *Achieving Compatibility with Handwriting Analysis, Volume 2; Handwriting a Key to Personality,* by Klara Roman, and *The Complete Idiot's Guide to Handwriting Analysis,* by Sheila Lowe.

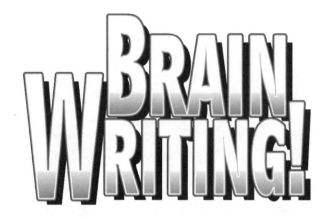

CHAPTER TEN

PRINTING

In the middle of the fifteenth century, printing began in Western civilization, but the Chinese, Japanese, and Koreans knew and used printing long before that period. In the twentieth century in the United States, school children were taught to print before they were taught cursive writing. Today, the majority of college students print rather than write. Our children have been taught to print, and today's society has reinforced our need to continue this discipline.

Often people say to me, "I don't write, I print." What do they really mean when they say that? I find that people THINK that they are printing. In actuality, their writing might be a combination of cursive and block or manuscript printing. This style represents a wish to be absolutely understood but contains a hidden message that we also desire to be in touch with our emotions and, subconsciously, will reach them by adding some form of cursive writing.

$$CURSIVE$$

When we print, we are calling on the resources of our subconscious mind. It is important for the printer to convey those thoughts clearly and concisely. The subconscious desire for clarity is conveyed by the printer every time she writes. It serves as her own private reinforcement.

The business world demands clarity of written expression. Usually, at the top of job applications we see clearly printed, PRINT—DO NOT WRITE. When we are concerned that our writing must be crystal clear, many of us print, even if the instructions do not definitely request printing.

When we print, we must leave a space between every letter. It takes longer to print than to write in cursive style. Writing then becomes a bit more tedious, because you must pick up the writing instrument every time you print a letter. Even so, it seems that many more college-age people today are printers. Is this due to a desire to control their emotions? Do they have a desire to sublimate their feelings?

It is possible that the writer may have found that his script is so illegible that printing becomes a necessity. People who must print for professional reasons include architects, engineers, draftsmen, teachers, and artists. If printing is mandatory during their workday, they will almost always print, even when they are not working. They have a desire for simplicity and will be direct in thoughts and actions.

Those who print only have a strong need for organization. They like to be in control of situations around them. They also have a desire to communicate.

It is interesting to discover when the individual started to print instead of writing cursively. Many times, I find it is easy for people to remember when they first switched to printing only. When they think back in time, they can even remember the situation that instigated their desire to print only. Usually, it stemmed from a need to be understood or to control emotional feelings. This often happened during the time in their life when they were teenagers or young adults.

When you print, it is possible to separate yourself from your emotions at the time that you are writing. On this page, try cursively writing your name, then try to print it.

Notice how you felt when you were printing your name versus how you felt when you were signing with your usual cursive meter. When you printed, especially legibly, you were controlling your thoughts. When you wrote cursively, you were more likely to be in touch with your emotions.

Printers often have very high self-regard. They seem to have more difficulty making long-term emotional commitments.

It is rare for people to print their signatures. Most people might regularly print or print script (a combination of print and cursive) the main body of their writing, but they rarely print their signature, unless specifically requested to do so. However, the following sample from Barbara Bush (wife of former president George Bush) shows her typically printed signature. Barbara Bush's sample displays a vanilla temperament that shouts to the world "what you see is what you get." It's as if she is saying, "This is the way I am, take it or leave it."

Barbara Bush, first lady.

Jacque Nasser, President and CEO, Ford Motor Co. His printing shows his desire to be completely understood. The underlining indicates self-reliance.

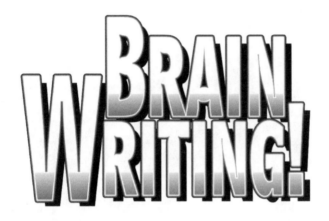

CHAPTER ELEVEN

BRAINWRITING! FOR SALES

Have you ever wished for a tool that you could use to instantly know details about your potential client? Brainwriting teaches you shortcuts you can use every day to better understand the personality of the people with whom you are dealing.

Understanding the hidden messages in your handwriting and the writing of your clients can be a career-enhancing sales advantage. Your new knowledge will help you to understand the strengths and weaknesses of others. You'll know the perfect approach to use on your clients. There will be no more guesswork about how best to relate to them. It will be like playing a card game—only you'll know every card in your hand as well as your client's. This new understanding will save you time and effort. It will greatly enhance your chances of making a real score. Your sales will soar, and your customers will be eating out of your hand.

Think of the advantages you will have in dealing with a husband and wife. You will know to which one of the two you should devote the most time. An important question in sales is often which spouse is the dominant one. One member of the couple may appear to be stronger on the surface but is really the weaker of the two. When you apply your knowledge of Brainwriting, you will have an advantage that you never before dreamed was possible.

The first thing a salesperson must do is to obtain a sample of her customers' handwriting. There are several ways to get one. The most obvious way is to observe their signatures—usually the first sign that you see. There are, however, other methods you can use. For instance, if you are selling something high-cost, such as a house or automobile, you could provide a HIS and HERS form sheet. Have each of the partners make a list of features that they would like to have in the home or car. Suggest the parties write the lists separately, so they won't influence one another's opinion. In addition to providing you with valuable handwriting information, your potential clients will be impressed with this novel, hands-on approach to house or car searching.

Ideally, it is best to get a sample of the thoughts of someone in whose writing you are interested. Here's a non-threatening personality game that you might find will help "break the ice" with the new people that you meet. Have them write the five traits that they value in a friend. Then, ask them to write two negative traits that would keep them from being that person's friend. The first five traits are indicative of their own personality. The next two are ones that they absolutely cannot tolerate. It's a fun game and will give you some interesting information that will help you learn to relate to them.

The following techniques will not make you a handwriting maven overnight. They are meant to be an aid to the person who wants to know something about handwriting analysis but does not have the time or inclination to study with intensity. The information will help you to understand the basic meaning of your writing and the handwriting of others. In addition, this new knowledge will provide some warning signals that will improve your ability to relate to anyone with whom you come in contact.

Here's what to look for in the writing that will give you insight into the needs and personalities of others.

THREE KEY ELEMENTS TO LOOK FOR FIRST

PSS

(P) PRESSURE

(S) SIZE

(S) SLANT

First, check the signature. You will have three major clues to tell you about your client's personality before you meet, and you will find them all in your client's signature. Look at the PRESSURE, SIZE, and SLANT of the signature or other writing.

PRESSURE

Heavy pressure

How heavy or light the person writes. (See examples in Chapter Five, Emotions and Feelings.)

Heavy writing indicates a deeply intense nature. These people carry feelings, hurts, or joys for a long time. Heavy-pressure writers feel so strongly about their beliefs that it can be difficult to reach them. Remember, they appreciate quality, not quantity. They absorb everything like emotional sponges. They are more materialistic and earthy. These people are probably self-assertive and determined. If someone prefers to always write with a heavy felt pen, you can assume that he or she is in the heavy writer category. These writers usually have a very strong will and seek to impose it upon others. Intense colors, like red, are most appealing to them. Look for expensive tastes in the writer who presses heavily on the pen or pencil. Such writers will sometimes go beyond their budgets to appease their desire for luxury. Appeal to their refined and extravagant desires.

Medium Pressure

Medium pen pressure is considered the norm between the extremes and indicates vitality and healthy willpower, but not to an overwhelming degree. Medium pressure is usually indicative of emotional balance and stability, if the baseline looks even and the writing does not seem too erratic.

Light Pressure

Light-pressure writers may be more relaxed and possibly more passive, usually more spiritual than assertive. They are often easier to convince than heavy-pressure writers. Writers who barely touch the paper with the point of the pen possess a delicacy of feelings. They exhibit less energy and, not being as physical, will often have more interest in people and social activity. They are far more tolerant and genial than the heavy-pressure writer. Their personalities are sensitive and impressionable and will often succumb to the dominance of the heavier writer. These writers can be undecided and more easily influenced. By the way, look for light-pressure writers to prefer soft colors, such as pastels.

SIZE

Observe how large or small the letters are. Those whose middle-zone letters measure approximately one-eighth inch tall are indicating that they are more practical and realistic.

Larger-size writers have a need to relate to people and to make an impression. They like or need to be seen and heard. They approach life with extroversion and extravagance. Material possessions are important, particularly if their script contains large lower loops. They will see the whole forest first, before they see the trees. If the writing is large in size, but light or medium in pressure, you're probably working with a person who is easy to approach and is receptive to a friendly demeanor. I find that the majority of people in the sales field have medium or large writing. When the large writer takes a whole page to write only a few words—stand back—give him or her plenty of room. He or she needs to take center stage.

Small writing (one-sixteenth inch or smaller) suggests that the writer sees everything in microscopic fashion. These writers will see the trees first, rather than the whole forest. They appreciate minute details, so be well prepared with facts and figures. Expect them to take the opposite viewpoint from a large-letter writer. They will be more introspective and reserved than the large or middle-size writer. In my opinion, few successful salespeople have exhibited small writing. It is possible for them to interact well with others, but they are most comfortable in a more exclusive environment.

SLANT

Observe the angle of the letters. A combination of the slant of the writing, plus the pen pressure, reveals the emotional foundation of an individual. The emotional foundation is the structure upon which the total personality rests. If you can learn to recognize the emotional structure of your client, you have already arrived at the top of the ski slope, and it's easy downhill skiing the rest of the way.

Most often, you only have time to briefly eyeball your potential client's writing. Such quick assessment takes practice. Ideally, take a few minutes to "play" with the slant. If you take the time, you will be more accurate and better able to gauge your potential buyer's emotional leanings.

How to Measure Slant (See Chapter Five)

Most people who are sociable, impulsive, and demonstrative have a slant toward the right. This includes seventy-five percent of our population.

Right slant: If the slant is far to the right, you can expect the person to be extremely impulsive, and it is a likely bet that he or she appreciates sincere flattery. You can assume you are dealing with a person who is emotional, so appeal to his or her emotions. The right-slanting writer is more sympathetic toward others and often more compassionate. When the writing falls far to the right, the writer tends to be more impulsive and will leap before he looks.

Vertical slant: These writers have their emotions under control. They are ruled by their heads more than their hearts. Shake hands with these writers quickly, and then step back in order to avoid getting into their "psychological space." These people can be uncomfortable if you get too close.

Leftward slant: When the writing leans to the left, expect the writer to be somewhat self-protective. He or she is usually not impulsive. A slant to the left indicates a person who is more withdrawn. Generally, he or she tends to think more logically. Give the person time to think it over before making the decision to close a deal.

Variable slant: This one is a red flag! If you observe an obvious slant variation from left to right in the same sentence or word, expect some surprises from this customer. This person has unpredictable mood swings and can withdraw into an introverted state when feeling insecure. When the slant is not fairly consistent or even, you have an individual who is not predictable.

If your client prints only, he or she will appreciate directness in you. (See Chapter Ten, Printing.) Try to be as concise as possible, and make an effort to let the person know that you are interested in not taking up too much of his or her valuable time. Perfection is usually most important to a printer, not only in the workplace, but also throughout life. Your client will not tolerate beating around the bush and expects you to get to the point as soon as possible.

So, you've checked the writing. The pressure looks medium, the size seems medium, and the slant seems pretty normal (somewhat to the right, but not leaning too far). No one pressure, size, or slant appears unusual. Don't panic! That's when you zero in on the telltale small t's and d's. You will glean much information by checking out the cursive d's and t's. As a matter of fact, if you can't tell much by looking at the rest of the writing, you can always use the t's to help you out.

If they are looped rather than retraced, expect the writer to be sensitive to criticism. The larger the loop, the stronger the sensitivity. Be especially careful when dealing with the writers of large, loopy d's and t's. You can bruise their feelings easily and (especially if the pressure is heavy) they might have difficulty forgiving you if they get the impression that you are criticizing them. Even if you think you are not being critical, they will feel otherwise.

If the d's and t's are retraced, they will prefer a direct approach and possibly resent what they perceive as a diplomatic or even condescending attitude. They much prefer a "tell-it-like-it-is" approach.

For more important information regarding t's, see Chapter Three.

Still don't have enough information? If you have time, check the lowercase i's.

The Lowercase i's

Observe the way the small i is dotted. A light, round dot indicates loyalty to a cause that the writer believes in, loyalty to a friend (or friends).

A slashed i shows irritation. If it is slashed to the right, it signifies irritation toward a person or others. (It's probably not irritation with you.)

If it is slashed downward, it shows irritation toward oneself.

A slash to the left indicates irritation toward something that has occurred in the past.

Note: The i slash trait can change and vary if the feeling of irritation lessens.

When the i is dotted to the right, expect impulsivity or impatience.

When the i is dotted directly over the stem, the writer can be detail oriented.

When the i is dotted to the left, look for a procrastinator.

Many times, an i dotted to the left is observed with a t crossing that does not extend beyond the stem. Then, look for major procrastination!

A circle above the i dot shows the individual is shouting "Hey, look me over." She has a need to be noticed and will often spend beyond her budget.

If a word ends in an upswing, the writer has the identical needs as the circle i dot. They want to be noticed by others. Give that person much attention.

Decisive Versus Indecisive

If the writing at the end of words is feathered or ends with sharpness, you might suspect that the writer is normally indecisive. You still might have a chance if you haven't closed the deal yet.

If the words end bluntly, or with a tiny dot, you can

assume that the writer is normally a decisive individual. When he or she says no, you can be sure he or she really means it.

Confusion of Interests

When the lower parts of words get tangled up with the next line, look for confusion of interests. This individual has so much going on, he or she doesn't know what to do first.

Sally has confusion of interests when many lines run into each other.

One last helpful hint: Be careful when you use this one! Is the individual a touchy feely person? In today's world, you want to use this information carefully. You might be totally misunderstood and, heaven forbid, even involved in a lawsuit. Your client might take offense. But, this book wouldn't be complete without sharing the touchy feely trait with you. When letters are constantly touching, it may indicate that the individual likes to touch and be touched. In other words, his or her tactile sense is well developed.

touch and close

The Communication Letters

O   The writer of a closed o will listen and watch before speaking.

O   Looped at the top: The writer's basic nature is secretive. This person will never tell all of anything.

U   Break at the top: When there is a break in the top, the individual is very talkative. Think of this person as needing to let the air out. (Helpful trait for a salesperson)

You will find that, not only is your knowledge of benefit to sales, but it will help you in any business endeavor.

Nowadays, because of computers, people tell me that they don't use their handwriting or that they print everything. That's nonsense! If you are in the habit of printing and you use your hand, it is handwriting.

You now have tools to assist you in using a new and simple method to help you make the sale. Thorough study of handwriting can become mighty complex, but if you follow this simple formula, you have information that can raise red flags for you immediately.

REMEMBER PSS TO MAKE THE SALE!
Check the Pressure, Size, and Slant.

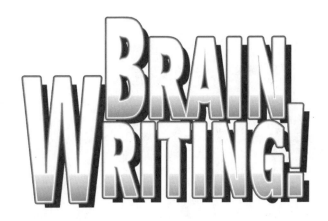

CHAPTER TWELVE

THE PERSONAL PRONOUN CAPITAL I

To me, the most interesting letter of all is the personal pronoun capital I. It is perhaps the most telling of all written letters. It is unique because, in English, it is the only letter of the alphabet that is symbolic of the self. It reveals the writer's ego and self-worth concepts, which, indirectly, also reveal the esteem with which the writer wishes to be regarded by others.

How you were nurtured is perhaps the most important aspect of your personality. We have much evidence of this by observing your capital I. Since the initial stroke is ordinarily upward from the baseline, we call the upper structure the mother image. This mother image does not necessarily have to be your brain's association with your biological parent. It indicates your feelings toward the person who was your maternal nurturer or who raised you.

The bottom part of the capital I includes characteristics that one usually associates with the father image. This image displays your feelings about the paternal nurturer in your life.

Mother influence

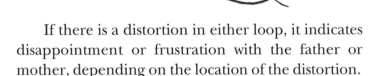

Father influence

If there is a distortion in either loop, it indicates disappointment or frustration with the father or mother, depending on the location of the distortion.

A small upper loop that does not begin at the baseline indicates a lack of nurturing as a child. It usually displays a poor ego image and a feeling of incompleteness. It often shows a feeling of not being able to measure up to the mother's expectations. If a distorted angle is displayed in either loop, it denotes hostility.

The structure at the base of the capital "I" is symbolic of the relationship to the father figure or the male nurturer in that writer's life.

When there is no overlapping of the two loops and wide spacing between the two, it is indicative of the writer's belief that the parents did not relate well to one another.

When angular formations are found in either the upper or lower structure of the personal pronoun "I" it is indicative of hostility toward the respective parent figure. If the angle is observed in the upper loop, it would reflect a form of hostility or anger toward the mother figure. If it is in the lower structure, then the hostility would be directed toward the father figure.

My father did not experience touching or physical demonstrations of love from his mother. As a result, he was unable to show physical warmth for any of his children. By the time I was three years of age, I was painfully aware of this and would do practically anything to get my father to physically demonstrate warmth to me. I would pretend that I was sleeping on the front porch so that he would have to carry me up to my bed at night. I yearned for that time. Mostly, though, my ruses rarely worked. Even when my father was quite old, he found it impossible to do anything but shake my hand when we first greeted each other. It became shockingly apparent to me that my feelings were graphically displayed by the way I cursively wrote the capital "I".

I'm not sure if I would advise anyone to change the way they write their personal pronoun I (to simplify, it will be called PPI). It is good to become aware of the way it is fashioned and perhaps to try to understand the meaning of why you make this stroke. It affected me in a rather intense way. Once I realized what my stroke meant, I endeavored to straighten out the stroke and make it more like the copybook version. Once this became a practiced part of my writing, I was shocked to see how it affected the way I related to my father.

Typically, I never forgot to send him a Father's
Day gift. The year that I consciously changed the way
I wrote my PPI, I did not send him a gift, for the very
first time. This went totally against my nature. Normally, I would not have thought of doing something
like that. In a way, for me, I guess it was somewhat
cathartic, but my father did not let me forget this fact
for a long time. I don't think that, consciously, I
wanted to make him feel bad, yet some part of me
did not want to recognize him, at least that year.

*President George W. Bush's personal pronoun I, dem-
onstrates an unfinished, or incomplete, relationship with his*

father. He does not exhibit a strong relationship with his mother, as well.

When the lower, or male nurturing, part of the PPI is curved, it tells me that the writer was very giving and lenient with the father. This personality trait carries forward in later years, so that it seems that the writer has a giving nature to all men in her life. It is especially apparent in the writing of females.

There are many ways to write the capital I.

The following are some examples of PPI and their meanings:

The Printed I

The mother has been more of an influence than the father has.

The father has been more of an influence than the mother has.

Single Stroke

The writer feels independent of both parents.

I hasten to add that after that one time, I always remembered special days. I examined my past, through my PPI, put it aside, and moved on. It was a part of history and no longer would I look back on it as a time of extreme childhood trauma. Yet, even today, I try to make my PPI look more like the copybook version. It seems to give me an inner strength when I take that little extra loop out of my PPI. It is my way of controlling my feelings about that part of my past. I try not to let that part of my life exert as much influence as it once did.

Understanding myself through my handwriting, has enriched my life. It can do the same for you!

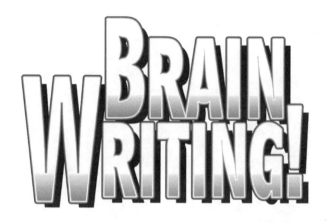

FREQUENTLY ASKED
QUESTIONS

FREQUENTLY ASKED QUESTIONS AND ANSWERS

Handwriting is essentially body language. Like other forms of body language, through electrical impulses (sent to the writing instrument, in this case), it is a manifestation of what's happening subconsciously.

Handwriting of individuals is as unique as fingerprints. WE ARE WHAT WE WRITE!

1. *How Much Information is Revealed by Handwriting?*

Almost anything, descriptively speaking. The major exceptions are age, race, ethnic origin, sex, and handedness. An analyst can assess personality and character to any depth the writer wishes.

2. *What can an Analyst Predict from Handwriting?*

Handwriting analysis is a descriptive science. An analyst can state a likelihood about someone's behavior, but will not predict what an individual will do with a given trait or group of personality traits.

3. *I Never Write the Same Way. Why?*

Handwriting is "frozen effect" and reflects the mood of the moment as well as the overall personality. Compare handwriting to the face. Although the expression is not always the same, the underlying features remain unchanged.

4. Can an Analyst Identify a Person's Good and Bad Traits?

Handwriting strokes are not necessarily "good" or "bad." Any trait can be used to one's advantage or disadvantage. An analyst might point out how a certain trait, if used in a particular way, might become an asset or a liability.

5. What Uses are Presently Being Made of Handwriting Analysis?

Personnel Assessment:

Employee selection/screening

Project compatibility

Executive recruitment

Outplacement counseling

Staff development assessments

Counseling:

Marriage/family

Individual therapy

Vocational assessment

Parent-teen relationships

Couple compatibility

Identifying questioned documents

Parole candidate assessment

Credit risk evaluation

Jury selection/screening

Analysis of historical documents

Graphotherapy

6. *Isn't Analysis an Invasion of Privacy?*

Not so, according to the United States Supreme Court!

U.S. v. Dionision (1973)

U.S. v. Mara (1973)

Gilbert v. California (388US263 18L.ED2d1178)

The U.S. Supreme Court found "Handwriting, like speech, is repeatedly shown to the public, and there is no more expectation of privacy in the physical characteristics of a person's script than there is in the tone of his voice."

As a result of decisions such as these, handwriting has come to be regarded as a form of body language, open to public assessment.

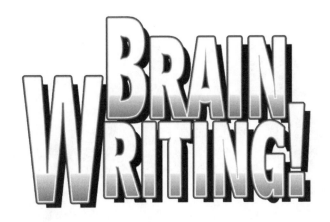

ABOUT THE AUTHOR

ABOUT THE AUTHOR

Irene Levitt is one of the foremost experts of handwriting analysis and founder of Handwriting Consultants, LLC. She is a charismatic speaker and consultant to business. Irene advises leaders in law enforcement and government agencies.

Her love of studying handwriting analysis led her to a master's degree in graphoanalysis. She has been an instructor in handwriting analysis, at the college level, since 1985.

Irene's people skills are legendary. A Music Therapist in Cleveland, Ohio, she worked with children who were emotionally ill. After moving to the Southwest, she became a casting director for major motion pictures.

Her company, Handwriting Consultants, LLC, provides:

• Forensic document examination

- Vocational analysis

- Criminal investigation

- Jury screening

- Self-awareness training

- Personality assessments

Additional Publications

"Brainwriting! For Sales" by Irene B. Levitt

"A Key to Your Personality Using Handwriting Analysis" (audiotape/handbook) by Irene B. Levitt

"Chocolate for a Woman's Soul" by Kay Allenbaugh (Irene B. Levitt, Contributing Author)

"Confessions of Shameless Self Promoters" by Debbie Allen (Irene B. Levitt, Contributing Author)

Contact the Author at:

Handwriting Consultants, L.L.C.

(v) 480-661-9199

(f) 480-451-6450

e-mail: Irene@Irenelevitt.com

web site: www.Irenelevitt.com

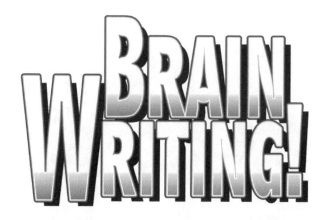

INDEX